Stoic Foundations

EPICTETUS' DISCOURCES BOOK 1

STOICISM IN PLAIN ENGLISH

Dr Chuck Chakrapani

The Stoic Gym Publications

Stoic Gym Publications
www.thestoicgym.com

Book Layout ©2017 BookDesignTemplates.com

Ordering Information:
Quantity sales. Discounts are available on quantity purchases by corporations, associations, and others. For details, contact the "Special Sales Department" at the address above.

Stoic Foundations/Chuck Chakrapani. —1st ed.
ISBNs:
Print: 978-0-920219-24-9
ePub: 978-0-920219-25-6
Mobi: 978-0-920219-26-3
PDF: 978-0-920219-27-0
17 18 19 20 21 22 23 24 25 26   1 2 3 4 5 6 7 8 9 0

Contents

The Reason Why

There are many excellent translations of Epictetus' Discourses in English. Even the nearly century-old translation by William A. Oldfather is very readable. So why a plain English version?

The most important reason for a plain English version is that the standard translations have an implicit obligation to follow the original text closely. Unfortunately, the original text was written about two thousand years ago in Koine Greek and *Discourses* was never edited for publication. In the intervening time, the meanings of words have changed. All this creates problems for the modern reader. Mostly, the standard translations look daunting. It took me about ten years from the time I bought a copy of Discourses to the time I ventured to read it from cover to cover. I found that the translations, as excellent as they might be, were not easy to read for several reasons such as:

- Dense layouts;
- Archaic and intrusive numbering system;
- Obscure references;
- Convoluted sentences.

- Non-descriptive chapter headings.

These may not deter scholars and academics, but common readers may not be so motivated. It is not the fault of the translators either. After all, translators are bound by the structure of the original text written about two thousand years ago. In general, they cannot deviate from it, even if the translation gets obscure in places. They can add footnotes and add explanations, but that calls for additional effort to understand.

So, a reader, who is not reading *Discourses* for scholarly purposes, can benefit immensely from a rendition that is true to the original text, but uses contemporary English. This is what this edition of *Discourses* does. More specifically this edition

- Uses modern English, simple words, and shorter sentences
- Rearranges a few sentences so they flow well
- Deletes obscure references when not necessary
- Attempts to use gender-neutral language from time to time to remind the readers that the principles are applicable to both men and women
- Adds clarifications in the text rather than in End Notes
- Occasionally tones down excessive references to God, gods, Zeus, and the like

I have also introduced some enhancements to the original:

- Descriptive discourse titles and subheadings within discourses.
- A summary of key ideas of each discourse at the beginning of the discourse.

- Clarification and occasional commentary in parentheses.

Through all these changes, I have tried to remain true to the spirit of what Epictetus was trying to say. To this end, I consulted several translations by eminent scholars while putting this edition together.

Is there a cost to all these changes? Probably. There might be some occasional loss in accuracy, especially when used for scholarly purposes – just as happens when a legal document is written in plain English. But, I believe the benefits of readability far outweigh the disadvantages of minor inaccuracies in places. As Saki put it so well "A little inaccuracy sometimes saves tons of explanation."

I would like to think that I have achieved my objectives but is for the reader to judge how well I succeeded in doing so.

A note on the titles in this series

The history of *Discourses* is well-known. Flavius Arrian, a student of Epictetus, transcribed the discussions Epictetus had with his students and visitors. He collected them in several "Books" (generally assumed to be eight, although only four survive). The books do not have specific themes and generally referred to Book I, II, III and IV. A.A. Long, however, believes that the first two books deal primarily with theoretical and methodological issues while the third and the fourth book deal with social and vocational issues.

I wanted to call each book by a name, rather than simply Book I, Book II etc. As there is considerable overlap of themes and topics among the four books, I looked for the dominant theme in each book and I believe I found it. Because similar themes recur in all four books, my judgement and choice of titles are inevitably arbitrary, but probably not too irrational.

How the books got their title

The first book of Discourses clearly lays out the foundations of Stoic philosophy of Epictetus. The first discourse is at the core of Stoic teachings. The book deals with the promise of philosophy, the importance of logic and reason, the law of life and how to live in this world. This book is titled *Foundations*.

The second book of Discourses deals with choices: caution vs. confidence, greatness vs. carefulness, good vs. evil, knowing vs. acting on our preconceptions, talking vs. practicing and several such choices. This book is titled *Choices*.

The third book deals with how to progress with our learning. How to train ourselves, what should be its main purpose, how to cope with impressions, how to bear illnesses, how we should not allow ourselves to be disturbed by news, and how to cope with failure and want. This book is titled *Practices*.

The fourth book has a lot to say about personal freedom. It starts with one of the longest discourses and it is on freedom. Freedom is one of Epictetus' basic themes and it recurs in many places in all four books. But freedom is expounded most prominently in the fourth book. This book is titled *Freedom*.

In addition, there is a summary of Epictetus teachings *Enchiridion*. There are scattered quotes called *Fragments* not found in *Discourses* which appear in books by other authors. Then there is the biography of Epictetus himself. To make this series complete in terms of Epictetus, I have included these materials in a fifth book. I call this book *Inspiration*.

Taken together, these five books make up the complete (available) works of Epictetus as well his biography.

Is this book for you?

If your aim is to understand *Discourses* without spending too much time and effort, you have come to the right place. If you are looking for a scholarly translation of *Discourses*, perhaps you should look elsewhere.

Stoic Foundations

Epictetus makes this bold claim "If you want, you are free. If you want, you will blame no one, you will accuse no one – if you want, everything will happen according to your plan." (Discourses 1.17.28). His teachings explore how we may achieve this unconditional freedom.

Stoicism, especially as expounded by Epictetus, consists of a few major themes that are repeated multiple times-sometimes in the same way, sometimes another way. The first book seems to be a particularly good summary of Stoic principles as taught by Epictetus.

Basic principles: A quick outline

Foundations revolves around ten themes, which are also repeated in other places throughout *Discourses*. These are:

1. *Concern yourself with only what is in your power.* Unlike other animals, we can reason. Reason enables us to not get carried away with first impressions but judge them properly. This is the only thing we need to do to live well.

Instead, we concern ourselves with so many external things – such as wealth, reputation, and the way we look – that are irrelevant to our living well. We have control over certain things in life but not over others. We make ourselves miserable by trying to control things that are not under our control and failing to control things that are. Train yourself to be concerned only with what is under your control and not with things that are beyond your control. [1]

2. *Be content to let things happen as they do.* The law of life is to live in accordance with nature. You are responsible only for things under your control. We always have the option of choosing what happens, as it happens. [26, 12, 25]

3. *Your thinking, not externals, drive your behavior.* We act according to the way we think. Our thinking drives our behavior. By changing our thinking, we can act differently. Never blame outside forces for your behavior. [11]

4. *Do not place value on external things.* It is not antisocial to be self-interested. But placing value on externals makes us become subservient to others and creates conflicts. We create our own problems by choosing to attach value to external things. We are social beings. External things are of no value. Our fear and envy are the result of valuing external things. External impressions can be deceptive. Good and evil come from our choices, not from externals. [19,25, 23, 24, 27, 29]

5. *Evaluate your first impressions using reason.* We get into conflict because different people interpret the same

impression differently. Placing value on externals results in contradiction and conflict. [20, 21]

6. *Don't give in to your anger or animal instincts.* People act in a way that appears right to them. So anti-social people such as thieves are misguided and deserve our pity, not hatred. We get angry at such people because we value external things (such as our property). [3, 18, 28]

7. *Always act your best. You can handle anything that comes your way.* No difficulty in life is unbearable if you can find a reason for it. So always act your best, even if you can never be as good as the best. Be diligent in your pursuits. Do not be upset if things don't happen the way you expect them to. Don't put yourself above others even when you have authority over them. Don't seek admiration. Be well-grounded. Be aware of God's gifts and be constantly thankful. Don't envy others. You have all the resources you need. Choose the right tool for the right job. For example, to combat a habit, choose a counter habit. You have no reason to complain. You have all the resources you need to cope with any challenge in life. Understand this and don't complain. God watches over us. Always have these principles handy. [2,10, 13, 21, 16, 24, 27, 6, 14, 30]

8. *Learn to think properly and logically.* Beware of rigid thinking. Learn logic so you can think logically. Learn what is important in each context and don't be carried away with things that are incidental. We need logic to understand what is true and what is false. [5, 7, 8, 17]

9. *Practice, not knowledge, results in progress.* Nothing happens instantly. Be patient. Challenging times reveal

what we are made of. Difficulties are opportunities for training. Play wholeheartedly or leave. Be steadfast in your practice. [4, 15, 24, 29]

10. *Only you can make you unhappy.* Remember your divine aspect and you have no need to worry. Only you – not others – can make you unhappy. Be a citizen of the universe. [9]

Understand What Is in Your Power

Key Ideas of this discourse

1. *Our supreme faculty is reason, because it can judge all other faculties, as well as itself. No other faculty can do that.*

2. *We control this supreme faculty of reason, and not of anything else. We are not even in charge of our own body, which may eventually fall ill or die, no matter how well we look after it.*

3. *Because reason is the supreme faculty, it is strong enough to lead us to freedom, happiness, and serenity.*

4. *The main job of reason is to manage impressions. This means we need to use reason to understand the truth behind our first impressions such as, "he is ungrateful," "she doesn't like me," "this is a disaster," and all our snap judgments, assumptions, and unexamined beliefs.*

5. *Instead of doing just this one thing that will lead us to freedom, happiness, and serenity, we become preoccupied with things such as our body, our friends and relatives, the weather, and the like. We become anxious.*

6. *We add misery to what cannot be controlled. When the weather is bad, we become unhappy about it, we add misery to an already "bad" thing. Being unhappy cannot change the weather but it can make you miserable.*

7. *Confine your actions to only things that are in your power. Train yourself not to concern yourself about things that are not in your control.*

Reason, our best gift

If you are writing a letter to a friend, grammar will tell you how write correctly, but not whether you should write that letter. If you study music, music will tell you whether something is melodious, but not whether it is appropriate to sing now. It is so with all disciplines. They cannot judge themselves. What can? The faculty of reason can.

Reason alone can understand and judge itself: what it is, what it is capable of, and the power it has. It can also pass judgment on other disciplines. What else tells us that gold is beautiful? What else judges music, grammar, and other arts and tells us when and how to use them? Not the gold or the grammar, but the faculty that evaluates such impressions – reason. Only reason can judge music, grammar, and other arts, evaluate their benefits, and tell us when and how to use them.

So, it is fitting that God has given us control over this excellent faculty – and only this faculty – that rules over all others: the ability to interpret impressions correctly. Why are the other faculties not placed under our power? We would have been given power over other faculties too, but we are on earth and bound to a physical body and material things. Therefore, we cannot avoid being limited by external things. Even our bodies are not truly our own, but just cleverly constructed to seem that way. Given these limitations, it is as if the God, because he could not give us control over our body, making it free of restraint, has given us a portion of himself.

Reason gives us the ability to act or not act and to desire something or move toward or away from it by properly judging our perceptions or impressions. If we pay attention to just this one thing, we will never be hindered, and we will never complain, flatter, or find fault. Does this seem like a small gift to you? Of course not!

Don't burden yourself with concerns

But instead of doing just this one thing right – managing impressions to arrive at the right conclusion – we burden ourselves with many things: Our body, our possessions, our brother, friend, child, and the like. We concern ourselves with so many things that they weigh us down. So, when dangerous weather prevents us from sailing, we become anxious and start fretting about reality:

"What wind is it?"

"North wind."

"When will west wind blow?"

"When it chooses, my good friend. You don't control winds."

"What should we do then?"

"Make the best use of what lies within our power and deal with it according to its nature."

"What is its nature?"

"Whatever God decides it is."

Don't add misery to what is happening

"But what if my life is being threatened and I am alone?"

"Do you want everyone's life threatened too? Remind yourself what is in your power and what is not. I should die; should I die groaning too? I am put in chains; should I feel miserable too? I am deported; what keeps me from going with a smile on my face?"

Face whatever happens

Whatever is within our power, no one can take away.

"Tell me your secrets."

"I refuse." This is in my power.

"I will restrain you."

"Only my legs. Even God cannot take away my choice."

"I will throw you in prison."

"Only my body."

"I will behead you."

"Did I ever claim that mine is the only neck that cannot be cut off?"

That is the attitude you should cultivate if you would like to be a philosopher. This is what you should think, write about, and practice every day. [Roman Senator] Thrasea used to say, "I would sooner be killed today than deported tomorrow." What did [the Stoic philosopher] Musonius tell him? "If you choose death because it is the worse of the two, how foolish! If you choose it as a lesser evil, who put you in charge of that choice?" It is foolish to have a preference when it is not under your control. Instead why don't you train yourself to be content and deal with whatever happens?

Don't become an obstacle to yourself

[The Stoic philosopher] Agrippinus said, "I will not become an obstacle to myself."

On hearing that he was being tried in the Senate, Agrippinus said, "Hope it turns out in my favor. But it is five o'clock. Time for my workout and bath."

Off he went to do his workout. When he was done, a friend came to inform Agrippinus that he was convicted.

"Death or exile?"

"Exile"

"What about my property?"

"You get to keep it."

"Let's go to Aricia and dine there."

This is how you should train yourself to think. When you think this way, what you desire cannot be restrained and what you want to avoid cannot be forced upon you.

"I must die. If now, I will die now. If later, I will dine now because it is dinner time. How? Like a person giving back what is not his own."

Think about this

I will not become an obstacle to myself. Discourses I.1.28. Agrippinus [CG/RH]

I must die? If now, I will die now. If soon, I will dine first because it is dinner time now. When the time comes, I will die. How? Like a person giving back what was not his own. Discourses I.1.32. Epictetus.

Act Your Best.
You Can Endure Anything

Key ideas of this discourse

1. *We can endure any pain that is inflicted upon us, provided we see a reason behind it. We should remember this and always act our best.*

2. *We can put up with anything (like an athlete enduring hard training) if we have a reason for it.*

3. *What you would endure depends on your character and what you value in life.*

4. *But, once you start placing a value on external things, you come close to a person who has lost all sense of their character.*

5. *Don't stop trying to act your best, even if you think you will never be as good as someone else.*

We can endure anything if we have a reason

A rational person can endure anything except things that are against reason. Take, for example, blows to the body. By nature, they are endurable.

"How so?"

"Watch how an athlete going through a rigorous training program endures punishment for not following the program, because he believes it is rational."

"What if I face capital punishment? Is that not unendurable?"

"Even when the punishment is very severe, if a person thinks it is reasonable under the circumstances, he would willingly subject himself to it."

We can observe that rational beings are drawn to what is rational and distressed by what is irrational.

We all have different ideas about what is rational

However, everyone has a different idea of what is rational and irrational, what is advantageous and disadvantageous, what is good and bad. Therefore, we need an education to tell us how to correctly identify what is rational and what is not rational according to nature; so, we can apply it to every situation we come across.

To do this we must consider two things: the value a person places on external things and the nature of the person involved. For one person, being a bathroom attendant to avoid pain and hardship could be rational; for another, doing such work under any condition could be irrational, even if he is beaten and denied food. Such a person may not even be able to tolerate another person submitting himself to such work.

The trade-off depends on your character

Which is the better: Security that comes with accepting demeaning work, or insecurity that might follow if you reject it? If you ask me this, I would say that it depends on what is important to you. What you would do depends on that.

If security is more important, then go and do the demeaning job. Did you say it is beneath you? It is for you to decide, not for me. It is you who know yourself, the value you place on yourself, and the price at which you would sell yourself. Different people sell themselves at different prices.

Florus [the financial officer of Judea under Emperor Nero] was debating whether to enter and contribute to the emperor Nero's festival. Agrippinus told him:

"If you are considering it, go and perform."

"Why don't you go to the shows yourself?"

"Because, I wouldn't even consider it."

Once you start placing a value on external things, you come close to a person who has lost all sense of their character. If you ask me, "Is death preferred or life?" I say, "Life." If you ask, "Pain or pleasure?" I say, "Pleasure."

"But if I don't take a part, I could be killed."

"Then go and take a part. But I will not take a part."

"Why?"

"Because you consider yourself as just another thread in a garment. So, you should give thought to acting like all the others. But I consider myself that small shiny purple band in that garment that gives beauty and luster to others. Don't tell me to be just another thread in the garment. If I did that, then how can I be the purple band?"

This is how another Stoic philosopher, Helvidius Priscus, chose to be different from others:

[On one issue, his views differed from Vespasian's. The Emperor approached Senator Helividius and asked him not to go into the Senate.]

"If you don't want me to go in, fire me. But as long I am a Senator, I must go in."

"Go in then, but don't give your opinion."

"I won't, if you don't ask me."

"But I must ask you."

"Then I must give my opinion."

"Do that, and I will put you to death."

"Did I ever tell you I was immortal? You do your part and I will do mine. It is your job to kill me, it is mine to die without fear. If yours to banish me, mine to go without grieving."

So, what did Helvidius achieve by this, he being just a single individual standing up to the emperor? The same thing that the single purple band did to the garment: set a fine example to others. Another person may have given in to the request of the Emperor, but the Emperor would not have tried to prevent such a spineless person anyway. The Emperor knows that such a senator would just go in and sit like a jug or simply say what the emperor wanted him to say, making it sound even more emphatic.

An athlete had to choose between having his private parts amputated and dying. His brother, a philosopher, asked him what it was going to be. The athlete declined to be amputated and chose to die with dignity. Someone asked whether he died like an athlete or as a philosopher. Epictetus said that the athlete died like a man. As someone who has participated in the Olympics and won. But another person could have chosen to have his head cut off even, if he could live. People do what is in line with their character.

"Come on, Epictetus, shave off your beard."

"I am a philosopher, I refuse."

"I will behead you then."

"Go ahead, if it will do you any good."

How do we know what is in line with our character? The same way a bull knows that it can stand up to a lion, when the herd is attacked. Don't you see that, if you have the power, you will be aware of it too? But no bull reaches maturity instantly. Nobility is not achieved overnight. We must endure winter training and take care not to rush into situations without preparation.

If you decide to sell your power to choose for security, decide at what price you will sell it, so you may not sell it too cheap. What is noble and exceptional perhaps belongs to others, people such as Socrates.

"Why don't we all act like Socrates then?"

"Are all horses swift? Do all dogs follow the scent?"

We should not stop trying because we are not the best

Should I neglect caring for myself because I am not naturally gifted? I may not be better than Socrates, but if I am not too bad, that's good enough for me. I may not be an Olympic champion like Milo, but that's no reason why I should neglect my body. I may not be renowned for my wealth like [the Emperor of Lydia] Croesus, but that's no reason why I should neglect taking care of my modest property. Of course, we continue to take care of things even when we know that we may never reach the highest degree of perfection in doing so.

Think about this

As soon as a person considers comparing and calculating the value of external things, he comes close to those who have lost all sense of their proper character. Discourses I.2.14. Epictetus

I shall never be a Milo, and yet I do not neglect my body; nor will be a Croseus, and yet I do not neglect my property. Discourses I.2.37. Epictetus [CG/RH]

Don't Become a Treacherous Animal

Key ideas of this discourse

1. *We have two aspects to us: animal-like and god-like.*
2. *The god-like aspect of us is our ability to reason.*
3. *Most of us are quicker to be animal-like than to be rational and god-like.*
4. *We should take care not to become like treacherous animals.*

You should be proud to be a child of God

If you genuinely believed that we are children of God, as you should, you would not think of ourselves as despicable or inferior in any way. If a king were to adopt you, there would be no end to your conceit. How come you are not proud knowing that you are child of God? In fact, you are not happy at all about this. Why?

We have two aspects to us: Divine and animalistic

Because, from birth, two elements coexist within us: a body that is common to all animals, and a rational mind and intelligence that we share only with God. Unfortunately, we are quick to identify ourselves with animals, even though it is miserable and mortal. Only very few of us identify ourselves with God, even though it is divine and blessed.

Everyone will necessarily deal with things according to their beliefs. So those that think that they are born for fidelity and respect, and are confident in their correct use of impressions, will not entertain any mean or ignoble thoughts about themselves. But the majority does the opposite and says, "Who am I but a poor, miserable piece of flesh?" Yes, the flesh is miserable. But you are better than the flesh. Why turn away from this fact and hang on to something that is mortal?

Take care not become a treacherous animal

Because of our relationship to the animal kingdom, some of us adopt animal-like qualities and become like wolves – noxious, faithless, and treacherous; or like lions – wild, savage, and untamed; in fact, most of us become cunning foxes. So, take care, don't take on the traits of treacherous animals.

Think about this

Take care that you do not become one of the roguish creatures. Discourses 1.3.9. Epictetus [CG/RH]

How to Know You Are Making Progress

Key ideas of this discourse

1. *To achieve serenity and peace of mind, you should*
    *   *direct your desires toward good things and away from sad things; and*
    *   *understand that you can achieve serenity only if you get what you want and do not get what you don't want.*
2. *You cannot make progress in these areas by simply reading books about them. You need to practice these principles.*
3. *As you make progress, you will be less inclined to indulge in self-pity but face anything that comes your way fearlessly and with dignity.*
4. *Be grateful knowing that you can achieve serenity and peace of mind.*

Reading books is not enough

You have learned from philosophers that

- you should direct your desires toward good things and away from sad things; and
- you can achieve serenity only if you get what you want and do not get what you don't want.

You are making progress when you completely get rid of your desires (or put them off for now) and direct your aversions only to things under your control. If you try to avoid things not under your control, you will fail sometimes and be unhappy.

Virtue promises happiness, an untroubled mind, and serenity. As you progress building virtue, you progress towards happiness, an untroubled mind, and serenity, no matter where the perfection of it is. Why is it then, after knowing this, we brag about our progress in things unrelated to this?

"What does virtue achieve?"

"A life that flows smoothly."

So, who is making progress? Someone who has read [the Stoic philosopher] Chrysippus' books? If virtue is no more than reading books by Chrysippus, then progress is nothing more than reading as many of his books as we can. By accepting this, we are saying that virtue produces one thing and progress towards it produces something different.

One can be sarcastic about this and say, "You can read Chrysippus all by yourself. Aren't you making great progress!" Why do you mock him? Why do you try to distract him from becoming aware of his error? Don't you want to show him the purpose of virtue, so that he will know what to work on?

"And what is that?"

"Working on your desire and your aversion."

Make it your goal to never fail to achieve your desires or experience things that you would rather avoid. Try not to make mistakes in exercising your impulse to act or not to act. Be equally careful before accepting an impression as true.

But first things first, look at the most essential ones. If you are constantly anxious and nervous while trying to be perfect, how have you made progress?

Don't show me your efforts, show me the results

Show me what you have achieved so far. If you were an athlete, I would want to see your shoulders. Don't tell me, "Look at all my training weights," but show me your shoulders. Enough of you and your weights; show me what your weights have achieved.

Similarly, don't tell me how thoroughly you have read the book *On Impulse*. Idiot, that's not what I am looking for. Show me instead what you learned from the book: how you exercise your impulse to act or not act, how you manage your desires and aversions, how you approach life, how you apply yourself to it and prepare for it. Are these in harmony with nature? If so, show me the evidence. Otherwise, be on your way. Don't comment on books or write them yourself. What do you gain by it? Don't you know books are cheap? Are you worth more than the cost of the book you are commenting on?

Don't look for your work in one place and results in another

Live what you have learned. What is progress then? If you can show me that you have learned that

- you are not controlled by things outside of you but by your choices
- you need to work on exercising choice that is in harmony with nature
- you are elevated, free, unrestrained, unhindered, faithful, and self-respecting
- if you are controlled by things outside your power, you cannot be free or faithful. You will be tossed back and forth and be at the mercy of others and they can thwart you
- when you rise in the morning, you (should) observe and keep these rules. You bathe and eat as someone who is faithful and honorable
- you (should) apply these principles from the moment you wake up, eat and bathe like a person of integrity, and apply these principles to everything that happens, just as a professional runner applies the principles of running to running or a professional musician applies the principles of music to singing.

If you can show me all these, then I will know that you are making progress and have not traveled in vain. But if all you are interested in is only reading books, I would advise you to go back home and take care of domestic affairs. You are here for nothing.

The purpose of studying is to learn to get rid of complaints, misfortunes, disappointments, and self-pity. You should learn what death is as well as what things like exile, jail, and poison are, so when something unfortunate happens, you can face it with dignity like Socrates facing his death sentence: "My dear Crito, if this is what pleases the gods, so be it!" and not saying "Poor me, an old man. Is this what old age is all about?"

Who says such things? Not just the humble, but Priam and Oedipus expressed such thoughts. And so, did all the kings of legend. What are tragic stories except descriptions of people who went after things that were not under their control, failed, and as a result, suffered?

The gift of serenity

If these tragic stories can trick us into learning that external things are outside our influence and therefore nothing to us, it will help us live in peace, free from disturbance. I wish this for me, it is for you to decide what you wish for yourself.

These principles on which serenity is based are true, Chrysippus assured us: "Take all my books and you will find things that are in harmony with nature give us peace of mind." We praise God: "How fortunate we are! Great benefactor who shows us the way!" We build temples and statues for things such as crops, corn, and vine we believe he has given us.

Aren't we forgetting to be thankful to the one who found and explained the truth that pertains not just to living but to living well? Who among you has ever erected a statue, built a temple, and praised God for that? We praise God and offer sacrifice for giving us wheat and wine. But he has produced such a wonderful fruit in a human mind that intends to show the true secret of happiness. Are we going to forget to express our thanks for that?

Think about this

These doctrines on which serenity and peace of mind depends are not false. Take all my books and you will see how true and in harmony with nature are things that give me peace of mind.
Discourses I.4.28. Chrysippus

Beware of Rigid Thinking

Key ideas of this discourse

Epictetus directed this Discourse primarily against the Sceptics – Academics and Pyrrhonists – who maintained that we cannot know anything for certain. In broader terms, this discourse argues against sticking to one's views, even when facts show otherwise. CC

1. *You can deny reality in two ways: by not seeing it and by denying it while seeing it. Denying something, knowing that it is true, is worse than not seeing it in the first place.*

2. *Denying reality consistently may pass for strength of mind, but it is no better than doing and saying whatever comes to your mind.*

3. *When a person does not see the contradiction in his thinking, we think it is sad. But when he sees the contradiction but still does not acknowledge it, we call it strength of mind. In reality, the latter is even more unfortunate.*

Denying reality

If a person denies what is obviously true, no argument would change his mind. We cannot reason with him. This is not because he is strong, or his teacher is week. But when a person contradicts himself in an argument, and becomes hard as a stone, how any can anyone argue with him?

Rigidity can come about in two ways: Either one's intellect is frozen, or one's sense of honor is. Such a person neither agrees to what is true nor leaves the argument altogether. Most of us will go to great lengths to avoid deadening the body; our souls, not so much.

Knowingly denying reality is worse

When a person does not see the contradiction in his thinking and is incapable of following an argument, we think he is in a bad way. But when someone sees the contradiction but still does not acknowledge it, when he has no sense of shame, we call it strength of character. In reality, it is even worse.

"Do you recognize you are awake?"

"No. No more than when I think in my dreams that I am awake."

"Is there no difference at all between the two?"

"No, none."

How can you argue with a person like this? What fire, what steel can I apply to make him realize that he has become deadened? When he knows and yet pretends not to, he is worse than a corpse. His sense of shame and moral feelings are gone or brutalized in any case. He is in a worse state than one who does not see the contradiction at all. Should I call this strength of character? Not unless I say the same about the character of lewd people who do and say in public anything that comes to their mind.

Think about this

One man does not notice the contradiction – he is in a bad way. Another man notices it, indeed, but is not moved and does not improve; he is in a still worse state. Discourses I.5.8. Epictetus [WO]

Don't Complain. You Have No Reason To

Key ideas of this discourse

1. *The universe is well organized, and everything is well coordinated. From this we can infer there must be a creator who created all this.*
2. *The grandeur of creation is all around us. We don't see it or appreciate it. Instead, we keep making bucket lists of places we must see before we die.*
3. *We have the resources to cope with every difficulty we face. Instead of using the resources we have been given to cope with the problem, we complain.*

The harmony of the universe: Why there must be a creator

You will find reason to praise providence in everything that happens in the world – provided you can see things in the larger context and if you have a sense of gratitude. Otherwise, you will not be able to see why something has happened. If you do see it, you will not be grateful for it. For example, think about colors:

- Colors are not enough; colors need vision to see.
- Vision is not enough; vision needs objects to see.
- Objects are not enough; objects need light to see.

Who thought of all these things – colors, vision, objects, and light - together and created them so they nicely fit into each other, like a sword fits into a scabbard? No one? When you consider how many things are created to be perfectly compatible with one another, it makes sense that it can't be random. Rather it is a creation of an artisan. When we see a sword and a scabbard together, we assume that someone made them. Why don't we assume a creator when we see vision and light together?

What about the desire to have sex and the human sexual organs created so compatibly for this purpose? Don't they demonstrate that there is a creator? Then, what about our minds? We get many impressions, but we choose among them. We combine different things in our mind, form certain ideas, and draw some conclusion. After considering all these complex mental processes, can you still discount the possibility of a creator? If you do, it is up to you to explain how all these things came about and how such wonderful artisanship came into being on their own, as random phenomena.

Do only humans have such skills? It is true many skills are special to humans, skills that rational beings need. Irrational animals have many of the same faculties as humans and use the impressions they receive through their senses. But they don't understand them, while humans do. Use is one thing, understanding is another. It is enough for animals to look after their biological needs: eat, drink, sleep, breed, and so on. Human beings are different. For us, that is not enough because we are given the faculty of understanding. To achieve our proper purpose in life, we need to act appropriately and methodically, in line with our nature. Otherwise we will fall short of our purpose.

Our purpose in life is to see and appreciate the wonder around us.

Each animal was created for a purpose. Some for production of cheese, some for farming, some to be eaten, and so on. To fulfil such functions, animals don't need to understand the impressions they receive and make distinctions among them. But we are brought into this world to witness the work of the creator. Not just to witness but to appreciate it as well. So, it is shameful for a human being to begin and end where irrational animals do. We should begin where they do, but only end in contemplation and understanding, and adopt a way of life in harmony with nature. So, take care not to die without being a witness to these things.

You travel long distances to see works of art and put many things on your bucket list. You think it would be unfortunate to die without seeing what is on your list. But to see the work of the creator, you don't need to travel anywhere. It's where you are standing right now. Don't you ever want to look at it, understand who you are, why you were born, and why you received the gift of sight?

Quit complaining and realize your strengths

You may say unpleasant and difficult things happen in life. Quite so. Suppose you get to a beautiful place. Then what? Won't you get hot? Won't you find it crowded? Won't you get soaked when it rains? Won't it be noisy? Won't you find other irritations? Knowing all this, you still go there because you think the beauty of the place is worth it.

Have you not received the inner strength to cope with any difficulty that may arise? Have you not been given strength, courage, and patience? Why then should you worry about what happens, when you are armed with these virtues and have the power to endure? What could possibly constrain, compel, or even annoy you? You don't see all this. Instead you moan, groan, shed tears, and complain.

"But my nose is running."

"What do you have your hands for, idiot, if not to wipe it?"

"But why should my nose run in the first place?"

"Why waste your time protesting? Isn't easier just to wipe it?"

What would have become of Hercules, if there had been no lion, hydra, stag, boar, or brutal criminals? What would he have done without such challenges? Clearly, he would have wrapped himself and slept.

"In that case maybe he should have created these challenges for himself – such as searching for a lion, a boar, and a hydra to bring them into his land."

"It would be madness to create problems for ourselves, so we can solve them. But the challenges that came Hercules' way proved useful tests of Hercules' nature and strength."

Now you know all this, appreciate all the resources you have. When you are done, say, "Let any difficulty come my way. I have the resources and a constitution given to me by my creator to deal with whatever happens."

But no, there you sit, trembling with fear about what might happen in the future and upset about things that are happening now. You blame God. How does such weakness help?

Yet God has given you the strength to tolerate trouble without being humiliated. He has also provided you a means to be free of constraint, hindrance, or compulsion, without having to fall apart. You have all these powers given to you which God himself cannot take away. Yet you don't use them. You don't even realize what powers you have and where they came from. You refuse to acknowledge your creator and his gifs. Some of you don't even acknowledge his existence.

My challenge to you

I am ready to show you that you have resources, strength of character, and resilience. I challenge you to show me what grounds you have to complain and be reproachful.

Commentary

Epictetus argues for the existence of God this way: Everything should have a cause. When you look and realize how coordinated the universe is, how smoothly it functions, and how well orchestrated everything is, it should be obvious to anyone there must be an intelligence behind it. This is the standard argument put forth even today by many as proof of

God's existence. A plausible argument perhaps, but it does not answer the question who created the intelligence that co-ordinates everything else.

From a broader perspective, however, this discourse is a call by Epictetus to his students to stop complaining, and understand they already have all the resources they need to cope with any difficulty that may come their way. They should be thankful rather than worried, anxious, or fearful. CC

Think about this

I undertake to show you that you have the equipment and resources for greatness of soul and a courageous spirit; you show me what occasion you have for complaint and reproach! Discourses I.6.43. Epictetus [CG/RH]

Deal with Arguments in a Logical Way

Key ideas of this discourse

1. *We can easily be deceived by arguments involving questions and answers as well as by hypothetical arguments.*

2. *During an argument, the initial premises may have subtly changed, giving rise to illogical conclusions. Unless you are trained in logic, it may be difficult to spot the deception.*

3. *Training in logic is important so we neither accept wrong conclusions nor act randomly and inappropriately.*

Arguments can have a bearing on how we behave

Some arguments change over the course of the discussion. Or, they can be hypothetical and end with a question. You may not be aware that such arguments have a bearing on how we should behave. We seek in every matter a virtuous path, so we may follow it. Therefore, a virtuous person would avoid question and answer sessions. If she is engaged in it, she would be indifferent to behaving casually and at random. If she accepts neither of these options, she needs to study more closely the topics of question and answer.

"What is the purpose of reasoning?"

"To establish what is true, reject what is false, and suspend judgment when we are not sure."

"Is it enough to know this?"

"Yes."

"Then is it also enough to know that you should reject counterfeit money?"

"No, it is not. You also need to know how to test for its being genuine, fake, or doubtful."

"So, don't you see, in reasoning too, spoken word is not enough? Is it not necessary to know how to test for what is true, what is false, and what is uncertain?"

"Yes, it is necessary."

What else? Because you need to accept the conclusions that are derived properly, you also need to know the rules of drawing conclusions: how they follow from one or more premises. Is it not then necessary to be able to offer proofs and demonstrations to others, and follow other people's proofs and demonstrations, so you are not easily fooled by cleverly disguised false arguments? Therefore, we believe that inferential and other forms of logic are important, and we study it.

Why logic is important

Sometimes, wrong conclusions appear to follow from what we believe to be the right premises. We cannot accept the wrong conclusion. Nor can we say that what we accepted earlier as right is wrong or that the logic is incorrect. What are we to do?

Examine the argument and see if the premises we accepted at the beginning have changed in some subtle way. If they have not, we have no choice but to accept the conclusion. If they have, we are under no obligation to accept the conclusion, because we no longer agree with the premises.

For example, a person who borrows money is a debtor, but not if he pays it back. The conclusion that he is a debtor was valid initially but not after he paid the money back. We need to examine premises of this kind because the very process of questions and answers can result in changing premises. This causes trouble to the ignorant who cannot see what follows.

What are we to do so we may not become confused and act inappropriately?

This is true of hypothetical arguments as well. Sometimes it is necessary to offer a hypothesis as the basis for an argument. Should you agree to every hypothesis as proposed? If not everyone, which ones should you agree to and which ones should you reject? Once you agree to a hypothesis, should you, forever, stand by the conclusions that follow? Or should you, sometimes, move away from them?

"Should you accept the results that follow from the hypothesis you agreed to and reject those that do not?"

"Yes."

"Suppose someone challenges you and says that they could prove something that's impossible using your hypothesis. Should a wise person avoid all dialog and examination with the challenger? After all, the wise person is the only one capable of proving that the challenger's arguments are false and nothing more than sophistry. Or will he engage in argument without caring whether he acts casually and randomly? If so, how can he be the man we imagined him to be?"

Without preparation, how can we maintain consistency in our arguments? If someone can show us that we can, then all our logical discussions are absurd and a waste of time. They serve no purpose and are at odds with what we think a good person is.

Why training in logic is important

Why are we still lazy, indifferent, and dull? Why do we give excuses and avoid training in logic?

"So, what? I haven't killed my father, have I?"

"No idiot, your father isn't there for you to kill. Instead, you are making this mistake, the only one you have the opportunity to make."

I once told my teacher Musonius Rufus, "It's not like I burned the capitol." He said "Idiot, the only thing missing here is the capitol."

Are there no other mistakes than burning down the capitol or killing your father? Is it not a mistake to use the impressions presented to you in a random and senseless way? To fail to analyze an argument to see if it is true or not, and to fail to see what logically agrees and what conflicts with your position – don't you see anything wrong with that?

Think about this

Establish what is true, eliminate what is false, and suspend judgment in doubtful cases. Discourses I.7.5. Epictetus [RD]

Distinguish the Important from the Incidental

Key ideas of this discourse

1. *Training in logic helps us spot incorrect and incomplete arguments, so we are not misled. Therefore, we need to train ourselves in logic.*

2. *Yet, if a person who is not ready for it is trained in logic, he may use it to demonstrate his superiority rather than use it the right way.*

3. *We need to distinguish the essential qualities that make a philosopher and not blindly imitate the incidental qualities we find in one.*

4. *What makes a person good? It is the quality of choices he makes.*

Different arguments can mean the same thing

The same argument can be presented in diverse ways. The following two arguments are variations of the same idea:

- You have borrowed from me and did not repay it; therefore, you owe me the money.
- You have not borrowed money from me and did not repay; therefore, you don't owe me money.

You need training in logic because not all arguments are stated in their complete form. Many arguments may leave out a premise [called enthymemes]. This is not a problem for a philosopher who is skilled in logic. She can still handle incomplete arguments as well as the same arguments presented differently. Because it is possible to vary the forms of arguments and arrive at the same conclusion, we should train ourselves in logic.

Why is it then that we fail to train each other this way? Even though we are not being distracted – not by me in any case – we are not making much progress towards achieving the right and the good. Under these conditions, what can we expect if we take on this additional project? It may not only distract us from studying more important matters but may prove to be the cause of pride and egotism.

Skills, in the hands of the untrained, can lead to pride

Logic and rhetoric can be powerful, especially when combined with elegance of language. However, if such skills get into the hands of the morally weak, there is the risk that they may become vain and presumptuous. How can we persuade such people they are supposed to use these skills rather than be used by them? Would not the morally weak ignore such advice and display their learning with conceit and pride?

Distinguish what is important and what is incidental

Just because I am a philosopher who happens to be lame, must you be lame to become a philosopher? Take care not to imitate a philosopher blindly. If a philosopher like Plato also happens to be strong and handsome, don't assume that you must become strong and handsome to be a philosopher. Did Hippocrates express himself eloquently *because* he was a physician?

Don't you want to understand what makes someone a philosopher and adopt those qualities, and not imitate accidental qualities? Am I suggesting that other positive qualities are of no value? No! No more than I would suggest the gift of sight is of no value. But if you ask me what makes a person good, I can only say it is found in the quality of choices he makes.

Think about this

If you ask me what human good is, I can offer you no other reply than to say that it lies in a certain quality of choice. Discourses I.8.16. Epictetus [RH]

Behave Like You Are Related to God

Key ideas of this discourse

1. *We are children of God. Therefore, we should stop identifying with a small place, and think of ourselves as a citizen of the universe.*

2. *You don't have to worry about the future. Even irrational animals don't. When you think that you cannot take care of yourself, you don't realize that you are having mean thoughts about yourself.*

3. *When you realize that external things have no power over you, you may want to end your life. But my advice to you is that God has stationed you here. Wait until you are called back.*

Be a citizen of the universe

If what philosophers say about our kinship with God is true, then it is only logical we are citizens of the universe, not of any country. When asked where he was from, Socrates never replied that he was from Athens or Corinth, but always, "I am a citizen of the universe." Why identify ourselves with the place where our body was dropped off at birth?

Those who know how the whole universe is administered know the first all-inclusive government is that of God and us. It is the source of all beings, going back generations upon generations, covering every creature ever born and bred on this earth. This is particularly true of rational beings since they alone are entitled by nature to be associated with God through reason.

Why not identify as citizens of the universe and children of God? Why should we fear any human condition? You may think if you are related to a king, or to some other powerful person, you can live safely and without fear. But you are related to God. Shouldn't you be free of grief and fear?

Be content being where you are

"But how can I feed myself if I am destitute?"

"Well, how about other poor people or runaways? Do they depend on their land, their servants, and silverware? Hardly. They rely on themselves and still manage to survive."

Are you, a philosopher and citizen of the universe, going to be dependent on others when you travel? Do you want to be more cowardly than irrational animals that are self-sufficient? Are they not provided with a mode of survival to live in harmony with nature? I'm an old man and I shouldn't be trying to persuade you not to think so small.

On the other hand, some young people among you may know your relationship to God; know that you are chained by your body, by your possessions, and other needs of your daily life. You may try to get rid of these things. But I would discourage you from doing so. It is your teacher's job to guide you. You should go to your teacher and say, "We no longer want to be tied to our body, possessions, and other things that bind us; we don't want to be associated with uncongenial people. All such things are indifferent to us. Here we have thieves, robbers, law courts, and people who think they have some power over us because of our body and possessions. Allow us to show them that they have power over no one."

If I were your teacher, I would say, "Friends, wait for God's signal for your release from service. Then go. For now, be content to be in the place he stationed you. Your stay here is brief, and it is easy enough to endure for people with your level of understanding. No tyrant, thief, or court of law can harm someone who places little value on body and possessions. So, stay here, don't depart without good reason."

No need to worry about what may happen

This is not how teachers and young students behave. Instead, as soon as you eat your meal today, you sit and worry about tomorrow's meal. I say to you, "If you get it, you will have it. If not, you will depart this life. The door is open. Why cry and complain? Why flatter or envy others? Why admire those with possessions, especially when they are powerful and quick to anger? What can they do to us? Or for us? Things they control are of no interest to us. What we care about, they cannot control. When we think this way, no one is our master. We cannot be made to act against our will."

How did Socrates feel about these things? Just like someone who knows the affinity between him and God. He was offered freedom if he refrained from engaging in the type of dialogues that he had been engaging until then, annoying the young and the old.

Socrates responded, "If one of your generals assigns me to a post, you would expect me to maintain and defend it and not quit even if my life is threatened. Not once, but a thousand times. Isn't it absurd that you expect me to abandon what God has assigned me to do and made it my way of life?" This is how a person with affinity to God would behave.

But we identify ourselves with our bodily organs such as our stomachs and guts. Our fears and desires are shaped accordingly. We become vulnerable to fear and desire. We flatter those we think can help us and fear those we think can hurt us.

Be self-reliant and appreciate what you have

A man, who was once wealthy and eminent, came to see me. He had fallen to tough times, lost everything, and asked me to write a letter to Rome on his behalf. I wrote a submissive letter. He read it and returned to me saying that he needed my help, not my pity, and that he faced no evil.

My teacher, Musonius Rufus, used to test me in a similar fashion. He would say, "Your master is going to afflict you with some hardship." When I answered, "Such is life," he would reply "Why, then, should I intervene with him when I can get the same things from you?"

It is silly and superfluous to get from another person what you can get for yourself. Since I can get greatness of soul and noble spirit from myself, why should I look to get an estate, money, or some position from anyone else? No, I will not be so insensitive to what I already have.

No one is ever unhappy because of someone else

If you are meek and cowardly, what else is left but to write letters for you as if you are already dead? If you don't realize that no one is unhappy because of someone else, you are just a dead body and a little blood.

Think about this

It is silly and pointless to try to get from another person what one can get for oneself. Discourses I.9.31. Epictetus [RD]

Be Diligent in Your Pursuit

Key ideas of this discourse

1. *We don't pursue our goals as diligently as people after power pursue theirs, even though our goals are highly worth pursuing.*
2. *All of us – both teachers and students – should stop being lazy and indifferent. We all should pursue our goals diligently.*

We are not diligent

If we pursue self-development as diligently as people after power pursue their schemes, we might get somewhere. I know someone who is older than me and works for the state as an official in charge of the grain supply. When he returned, being out of power for a while, he talked to me about his former life with disdain and said,

"I would give myself exclusively to a life of peace and tranquility from now on. Not much time left of my life."

"I don't believe you. Your resolve will last only if you don't have access to power. The moment that happens, you will forget all this."

"Epictetus, if I ever put one foot in the palace, think of me whatever you like."

How did he act? Even before he entered Rome, he received his letter of appointment. He immediately forgot all he'd said and has not given it a thought ever since. He is piling one encumbrance on another. I should be glad he passed through this place and talked to me. He made me feel as clever as a prophet compared to him.

We tend to be lazy

Am I saying that he is like an animal unfit for action? Not at all. But why don't we act? Look at me. In the morning, I remind myself which author I should be reading with the students. Then I tell myself, "Who cares if the student reads this or that author. First let me get my sleep."

All pursuits are not of equal value

And yet how can the business of the state compare to ours? If you look at what they do, you will see. What do they do except vote on a resolution and then huddle together discussing some means of making a living? Is there any comparison between the requests they receive, such as, "Please allow me to export some grain," and the requests we receive, such as, "Please teach me Chrysippus so I may learn how the universe works, where we rational beings fit in it, and where good and evil lie." Are these two things equal? Is it as shameful to neglect one as to neglect the other?

It is not just us teachers who are lazy and indifferent. You young people are even worse. When we see youngsters at play, we join them. We would be even more interested in joining them in serious study if they were wide awake and keen on studying.

Think about this

If we had applied as heartily to our own work as the old men at Rome do to their schemes, perhaps we too might have achieved something. Discourses I.10.1. Epictetus [CG/RH]

Know That Your Opinions Drive Your Behavior

Key ideas of this discourse

1. *Not knowing right from wrong – what is natural from what is not – is a great shortcoming.*
2. *We cannot assume that a behavior adopted by most people is necessarily in accordance with nature.*
3. *Our opinions, not externals, are the cause of our actions. If we think differently, we will act differently.*
4. *Therefore, when something happens that makes you unhappy, don't investigate external things to decide what caused your unhappiness. Examine your judgments about them that led you to your unhappiness.*

Acting naturally means acting correctly

A government official came to visit Epictetus. After some small talk, Epictetus asked:

"Do you have a wife and children?"

"Yes, I do. But I'm miserable"

"How so? People don't marry and have children to become miserable, but to be happy."

"I'm anxious about the children. When my little daughter fell ill, I couldn't bear to be with her. I went off until I was told her condition had improved."

"Well, did you act correctly here?"

"I acted naturally."

"If you can convince me that you acted naturally, then I am prepared to show that you acted correctly."

"That's what most fathers do."

Majority behavior may not be the correct one

"I know many fathers act this way. But is this correct? Would you then say doing wrong is in in accordance with nature because most of us do wrong? It is like saying tumors are good for the body, because they happen. So, tell me, exactly how the way you acted is in accordance with nature?"

"I don't think I can. Why don't you show me why it is not natural and shouldn't happen?"

"How would you distinguish between black and white?"

"By sight."

"How would you distinguish between hot and cold, or hard and soft?

"By touch."

"We are debating natural and unnatural, right and wrong. How do we distinguish those?"

"I don't know."

"Is this a minor shortcoming – not knowing right from wrong, what is natural from what is not?"

"No, a great one."

"Is everything that some people judge to be good and proper, rightly judged? For example, Jews, Syrians, Egyptians, and Romans have different views on food. Can all of them be right?"

"How could they?"

"So, if one of them is correct, the others are not. Likewise, where there is ignorance, there is a need for teaching and learning. Once you are aware of this, you will devote all your attention to discovering the standard that discriminates between what is natural and what is not; and then apply this knowledge to specific instances."

How to distinguish what is natural from what is not

Epictetus continued. "Let me start with this. Is family affection good and natural?"

"Yes."

"So, can family affection be good and natural, while what is reasonable is not good?"

"Of course not."

"So, whatever is rational will not conflict with family affection. Because if they were, one would agree with nature while the other would not. The two things cannot be in conflict."

"Indeed"

"Leaving your child's side when she is sick is not rational, even if you argue otherwise. But let's see if it is consistent with family affection. Was it right for you, when you love your child, to leave her? Let's consider her mother. Does she love the daughter?"

"Yes, of course."

"Would it be all right then for the mother to leave your daughter?"

"No."

"How about the nurse and the attendant? Do they love the child?"

"They do."

"Should they also have left her?"

"Certainly not."

"According to your logic, it is also all right for them to leave the child. The result is, because you all love her so much, the girl would have been left completely alone and helpless and probably would have died in the company of people who didn't particularly care for her."

"I hope not."

"Is it not unfair to claim that people who love the child as much as you do should not be permitted to do what you did because of your professed affection?"

"It's absurd."

"If you were sick, would you want your family, your wife, children, and others to be so loving as to walk away from you and leave you all alone?"

"No."

"Would you want them to be so loving that because of their love, you would always suffer your illness in isolation?

If you would like your enemies to leave you alone, would you wish that they loved you so much as to leave you alone? From all this we can only conclude that what you did was no act of affection. Can you think of anything that induced you leave your child?"

"How is that possible?"

There is but a single reason for our actions

Your motive could be compared to that of a person at a race course who covered his face while his favorite horse was running. When it unexpectedly won, he fainted.

A precise explanation may be out of place here. For now, it is enough to be convinced that you will not find any cause outside of yourself. The same is the reason to do or not do something, to say or not say something, to be elated or depressed, to pursue or avoid something. The same is the reason for you listening and me speaking now.

We act according to the way we see things

We believe that the way we see things is right. If we saw things differently, we would act differently, in line with what's right and wrong. This is the reason some people choose to grieve intensely when a friend or companion dies while others don't. You chose to leave your daughter because you thought it was a promising idea at the time. If you had stayed with her, it would be for the same reason. You have decided to return to Rome because it seems right for you; but, if you change your mind about it, you will not go.

In other words, death, pain, exile, or anything else external isn't the cause of our actions. Rather it is our judgments about those things.

"Have I convinced you of this?"

"You certainly have."

Never blame the externals

Results are related to causes. So, from now on, whenever we do anything wrong, we will not blame others; but only our opinions on which we based our actions. We will try to root out wrong opinions by applying even more care than we do to eradicating tumors and infections from our body.

Similarly, let's realize what we do right also is based on our opinions. We now know that if we did not have that opinion, we would not have acted the way we did, based on that opinion. Therefore, the results you get are solely based on the cause – your opinion. You are the master of your opinion. It has nothing to do with others. We will not blame our servant, neighbor, spouse, or children as the cause of anything bad that happens to us.

From this day, we will not investigate or inquire into the nature or condition of anything – be it of those who work for us, our horses, or dog. We will only investigate our opinions and judgments. This means you should be willing to become a life-long student, even if others laugh at you. You should focus only on examining your judgment. And this cannot be done in a single hour or a single day.

Think about this

From this day forward then, whenever we do anything wrong we will ascribe the blame only to the judgment from which we act. Discourses I.11.35. Epictetus [CG/RH]

Be Content to Let Things Happen as They Do

Key ideas of this discourse

1. *There are many views about God. Our view is that God exists and cares about what happens to everyone.*
2. *You are free if everything that happens to you happens according to your choice and not contrary to it.*
3. *Everything will happen according to your choice when you learn to will that things happen as they do.*
4. *You have the resources to cope with anything that might happen to you.*
5. *You are responsible for only those things under your control. You are released from all other responsibilities.*

Different views about God's existence

There are different views of God:

- God doesn't exist at all.
- God exists but doesn't care about anything.

- God exists and cares, but only about heavenly matters, not about earthly ones.
- God exists, and cares about what happens on earth, but not about individuals.
- God exists, and cares about everything, including individual welfare.

Socrates accepted the last view, when he said, "Not a move do I make that you do not see."

Which is the correct view?

Which one of these views is correct? Let's examine.

If there is no God, or if God exists and does not care about anything, what is point of the instruction, "Follow God?" If God exists but does not care about what happens on earth and especially to individuals, then again there would be no purpose in following God. Therefore, an intelligent person examines all these arguments and submits his mind to the ruler of the universe, just like good citizens submit to the laws of the state.

If you want to learn, you should come with the following questions:

- How can I follow God in everything?
- How can I live in happiness under divine governance?
- How can I become free?

What it means to be free

You are free if everything that happens to you happens according to your choice and not against it.

"Is freedom madness, then?"

"Freedom and madness are incompatible with each other."

"But I wish that anything that I desire happens as I wish."

"You are crazy. You have lost your senses. Don't you know that freedom is a good and valuable thing? To wish that unconsidered things happen at random according to your desire is not valuable, it is shameful."

If you want to print the name Dion, you were taught to choose the right letters in the right order: D-I-O-N. What about music? The same is true. What about other arts and sciences? The same thing. Otherwise, there would be no purpose knowing anything. So how do you expect the greatest and highest matter of all, freedom, be random?

"What is the true instruction, then?"

"Learn to will that things happen as they do."

"And how do they happen?"

"As God wills."

He willed there be summer and winter, abundance and famine, virtue, and vice, and all such opposites for the sake of harmony in the universe. For us he has given a body and its parts, property, and friends. Knowing all this, you should approach learning not to alter the facts, which is neither possible nor desirable, but to see them as they are, so we may remain harmonious with things as they happen.

Reframe your thinking to be in accord with nature

Avoiding others is not possible. Nor do we have the power to change others. Then how do we deal with them? By understanding that people will act as they please, but we will act in accordance with nature.

That's not what you do though. You gripe and protest. When you are alone you say you are lonely. When you are with people, you find fault with them, even if they are your parents, children, spouse, and neighbors. What you should do instead is this: When you are alone call it peace and freedom; when you are in company, instead of calling it a crowd and being annoyed, call it a festival. Learn to enjoy it.

Misery is the penalty for not being in accordance with nature

What is the penalty for not accepting the things the way they are? To be just the way you are: miserable when alone and unhappy when with others. There is no need to throw you in prison, you are already in one. Whatever place you are in, if you are there against your will, you are in prison. But even if you are in prison, if it is by your will, then you are free. This is the reason Socrates was not imprisoned, because he was there willingly.

So, what if my leg is crippled? It's just an insignificant leg. Do you want to blame the universe for it? Why not joyfully surrender your entire body to the one who gave it to you? Do you want to be angry and discontented with God, who designed everything at the time of your birth? Don't you realize your insignificance in the larger scheme of things? That is about the body. But, as far as reason is concerned, you are on par with God. The greatness of reason is not measured by size but by the quality of its judgments. So, would you rather not be equal to God?

You can cope with any situation

Are you discontented because of the parents you have? How would it have been possible for you to exist before your parents' time and say, "Let such a man make love to such a woman, so I can be born in a certain way." No, it would not have been possible. It was necessary for your parents to have existed before you were born.

"How so?"

"It's just the way things are."

"If so, don't you have any remedy?"

Well, if you don't know the purpose of sight, you might close your eyes as a beautiful painting passes by you and feel miserable. Are you less miserable not knowing you have the resources to cope with anything that may happen to you? You are given the faculty to cope with things. But you turn away from it at the very time you need it. Why don't you give thanks to God, knowing that he made you superior to everything that is not under your control and made you accountable only for things that are?

You are responsible only for the things under your control

You are released from all accountability to your parents, brothers, property, life, and death. What are you accountable for then? Only for things under your power, and the proper use of impressions. Why are you then worried about things not under your power? You are simply creating problems for yourself.

Think about this

You forget the virtues of character you have in reserve, just when problems they can control present themselves, and you could use their help. Discourses 1.12.31. Epictetus [RH]

Act Rationally to Please God

Key ideas of this discourse

1. *Do not be upset if things don't happen the way you expect them to.*
2. *Remember not to put yourself above others, even if you have authority over them.*

Act in a pleasing way

Someone asked Epictetus: "How one can eat in a way pleasing to God?"

"If you ate with restraint and self-control, would that not be pleasing to God? You ask the waiter to bring hot water. She brings lukewarm water or even totally ignores you. If you don't get angry then, would it not be pleasing to God?"

"How can I tolerate such people?"

"The same way you would tolerate your brother, who has the same God for a father. Why do you have to put yourself above him?"

If you are placed in a position above others, are you going to behave like a tyrant? Won't you remember who you are and who you are placed above? They are your kin, siblings by nature, and descendants of the same God. You pay for their services, you say? You are concerned with the laws of the earth, laws of the dead, not laws of God.

Think about this

If you are placed in a position above others, are you automatically going to behave like a despot? Discourses I.13.4. Epictetus [RD]

God Watches over Us

Key ideas of this discourse

1. *If we see the unity of everything around us and see how everything in nature is coordinated, then it is easy to understand that God watches over everything that we do.*
2. *God has provided us with a personal guardian who looks after us all the time.*
3. *Therefore, we need to swear allegiance to God.*

There is unity in everything we see

Someone wanted to know how one can be sure that God watches over each of our actions. Epictetus asked:

"Do you not see unity in everything?"

"I do."

"Don't you think that things on earth feel the influence of heaven?"

"Yes."

How else could things happen with such precise regularity, if God weren't issuing orders? He orders plants to bloom and they bloom. He tells them to bear fruit and they do so. When he tells them to ripen, they ripen. Again, when he tells them to drop their fruit, shed their leaves, lie dormant in winter, they obey. How else to explain the waxing and waning of the moon, coming and going of the sun, and changes and fluctuations on earth? If plants and our bodies are so influenced, wouldn't it be truer of our minds? If our minds are so intimately connected with God and a part of his being, would he not be aware of their every motion?

To know how god works, observe life

You can understand in detail how God works by observing your daily life. You can process a wealth of thoughts and impressions simultaneously. Some of these impressions you accept, some you reject, and yet others you suspend judgment on. Your mind can store many of these impressions from a variety of objects. Based on all these, the mind forms ideas in line with specific impressions. This is how we form memories and create arts and sciences.

If we can do all this, is not God capable of surveying all things, being present in everything and communicating with everything in the world? The sun illuminates a large part of the universe, leaving only a small part covered by the shadow of the earth unlit. Can't he, who made the sun – which is but a small part of the universe and causes it to turn, see everything that goes on?

"But I cannot understand all these things at once."

"Did anyone say that you have the capacities that are equal to God's? No!"

Yet he has provided every one of us with a personal guardian deity to stay with us and look after us. This guardian never sleeps and cannot be distracted. Is there a better or more vigilant guardian God could have given us? Whenever you shut your door and turn off the lights, don't say to yourself that you are alone. You are not. God is inside and so is your personal deity. They don't need light to watch over you.

We need to pledge allegiance to God

You need to swear allegiance to this God, as soldiers do to the king. If they want to be paid, they must put the king first. You have chosen to receive favors and blessings for free. Why won't you swear a similar allegiance to God? If you have already done so, why won't you abide by it?

"What must you swear?"

"You swear that you will not disobey, accuse, or find fault with God's gifts and that you will not shrink from things that are inevitable."

"Are these oaths similar?"

"Not at all. The soldiers swear to honor just the king; but we swear to honor, above all, our true selves."

Think about this

If plants and our bodies are so intimately linked to the world and its rhythms, won't the same be true of our minds – only more so? Discourses I.14.5 Epictetus [RD]

Nothing Happens Instantly

Key ideas of this discourse

1. Philosophy does not promise anything that is not under your control but seeks to preserve your governing part in accordance with nature.

2. However, the human mind does not come to fruition quickly. You must be patient because nothing important happens in an instant.

Philosophy does not promise anything that's not under your control

A man came to Epictetus and wanted to know how to get his brother not be in bad terms with him. Epictetus told him that philosophy does not promise to get us anything outside of our control. Otherwise it would be taking on matters that do not concern us.

"As wood is the material for the carpenter, as marble is for the sculptor, so is the art of living for each individual."

"How about my brother's life?"

"It is *his* art of living. But as far as you are concerned it is as external to you as land, health, and reputation. Philosophy has nothing to say about these things. However, it tries to preserve the governing part inside of you in accordance with nature at all times"

"Then, how do I stop my brother being angry with me?"

"Bring him to me and I will tell him. I have nothing to say to you about his anger."

"Tell me this then. How can I stay true to nature, even when he refuses to reconcile with me?"

Nothing happens in an instant

"Nothing important happens in an instant. Even grapes and figs take time to ripen. If you say you want a fig right now, I will ask you to be patient. First let the tree blossom and bear fruit. And then, let the fruit ripen. If the fig tree is not brought to maturity instantly or in an hour, how do you expect the fruit of a human mind to come to fruition in such a brief time, and so easily? I tell you, don't expect any such thing."

Think about this

Nothing important comes into being overnight ... be patient.
Discourses I.15.7. Epictetus [RD]

Give Thanks Constantly

Key ideas of this course

1. *The evidence of God's work is everywhere. You can see it even in insignificant things.*
2. *Instead of giving thanks for the gifts we have received, we keep complaining.*
3. *Let's constantly give thanks for the gifts we have received.*

Why animal needs are provided for

Animals are provided with all the things they need to maintain their body – food, drink, a place to lie down. Not only that, they don't need shoes, beds, or clothes while we humans do. Don't be surprised by this. Animals are born to serve others and not themselves; therefore, they are not burdened with additional needs.

Imagine what it would be like if we had to worry about finding clothes and shoes, or food and drink for sheep and donkeys, in addition to providing these essentials for ourselves! But just as soldiers report to their generals ready for service, equipped with shoes, clothes and armor, so nature has created the animals already prepared and equipped, so they require no further care. It would be too much to expect the commander to have to equip them personally.

The result? A small child, armed with nothing more than a stick, can control the entire flock of sheep.

Give thanks that it is so

We don't see all this and give thanks. Instead we complain about our condition. If we even had a tiny amount of gratitude or respect, the lowest of creations would be enough for us to admit the existence of providence. I am not even talking about wonderful things for now but simple things: milk is produced from grass, cheese is produced from milk and wool can grow out of skin. Who created or thought of these things? "No one," some say. What stupidity and shamelessness!

Consider how nature makes everything useful

Ignore the primary features of nature. Just consider the secondary ones. Is there anything less useful than hairs that grow on a chin? But nature found an excellent use for it too, enabling us to distinguish between a man and a woman even from a distance:

"I am a man. Approach me and deal with me as a man. Nothing else is needed. Just notice nature's signs."

Similarly, nature has provided a softer voice to women and they are deprived a beard. Of course, we could announce ourselves, "I'm a man!" or, "I'm a woman!" But consider how proud and becoming these signs are. They are more attractive than a cock's comb and prouder than the lion's mane. We should safeguard these signs God gave us.

Are these the only signs that providence gave us? Hardly! In fact, there are no words adequate to do justice to them or praise them. If we had any sense, there is nothing better we could do with our time than praise God and appreciate his good works, publicly and privately and remember the benefits he bestows upon us. We should praise him even when we are busy digging, ploughing, or eating.

- "God is great – he has given us these instruments to work on the earth."
- "God is great – he has given us hands, a mouth, and a stomach."
- "God is great – he has given us the ability to grow unconsciously and breath in our sleep."

This is what we ought to sing on every occasion, celebrating the ability he has given us to understand and use his works systematically. This is the greatest and the holiest of hymns.

But most of you have become blind. Someone must fill this role and praise God on your behalf. What else can a lame old man like me do except sing God's praises? If I were a nightingale or a swan, I would sing like either of them was born to sing. But I am a rational being, so my song is a hymn. This is my job and I will do it. I will continue to sing if I am permitted. I invite you to join me.

Think about this

We neglect to give thanks ... then complain to God concerning our own condition. Discourses I.16.6. Epictetus [RD]

Realize the Importance of Logic

Key ideas of this discourse

1. *We need to study logic to understand what is true and what is false and to analyze ambiguous arguments.*

2. *We study philosophers not to master their works, but to understand what they are trying to teach us. We are interested in the interpretation, not in the interpreter.*

3. *If you want it to be so, you can be free; you need blame no one, accuse no one and everything will happen according to your plan.*

Why we should study logic

"Reason analyzes and coordinates everything. Therefore, reason should not go itself unanalyzed."

"By what? By itself or by something else?"

"It cannot be by something else, because there is nothing superior to reason. If it is some form of reason, what will analyze that reason? If it is by something else still, then that something has to be analyzed by yet another something and the process can go on forever."

"True. But it is more urgent to attend to our judgments and the like."

All right then. I can talk about them instead. But if you then say to me, "I am not sure if your arguments are true or false," or ask me to clarify one of my ambiguous expressions, I am likely to say, "But it is more urgent to attend to our judgments and the like."

Therefore, Stoics put logic first, just as we agree on a standard of measurement before measuring a quantity of grain. If we don't establish standards for measuring weight and volume, how are we going to measure or weigh anything? It's the same here: if we don't fully understand and refine the instrument that analyzes and understands other things, how can we hope to acquire precise knowledge about them?

"But the measuring bowl is made of wood and bears no fruit."

"It measures grain though."

"But matters of logic can also be unproductive."

Well, we will see about that. Even if you are right, logic has the power to distinguish and analyze other things, acting as weights and measures for abstract matters.

Who says so? Is it only [the Stoic philosophers] Chrysippus, Zeno and Cleanthes? Does not [the Cynic philosopher] Antisthenes say it too? Did Socrates not say that the beginning of education is the examination of terms? Did not Xenophon say that Socrates began his talks with examining the terms to find what they mean?"

"Is this the ultimate achievement then, understanding philosophers like Chrysippus?

"No one is saying that."

"What then is the ultimate achievement?"

"To understand the will of nature. Can you understand it all by yourself, without help? If so, you don't need anyone else. Clearly you could use help because we all make mistakes. If you already knew the truth, others would be able to see it your flawless behavior."

"But I don't understand the will of nature. Who would explain it to me? Someone says that Chrysippus can, so I go to find out what he says. But then I have trouble with one of his passages. I ask someone to explain the explanation, as if it were in Latin. What right has the commentator to feel superior? Even Chrysippus himself has no right to feel superior if he only explains the will of nature but does not follow it."

Philosophers are not important, what they say is

It is not Chrysippus per se we need, but his writing to the extent it helps us understand nature. We don't need prophets for their own sake but through them we can divine the future and understand the signs sent by God. We don't need the victim's entrails for their own sake, but for the signs they convey. We don't worship the crow or the raven but the God who communicates through them. Therefore, I come before this diviner and interpreter and say, "Please examine the victim's entrails; what are they telling me?" After carefully spreading and examining them, he says, "You have a will incapable of being restrained or compelled." Let me show this starting with assent.

"Can anyone stop you from agreeing with what's true?"

"No."

"Or force you to believe what is not true?"

"No."

"Clearly, then, in this area your will cannot be forced or hindered. Now let's look at desire and impulse. It is just the same. One impulse can be overcome only through another impulse. One desire or aversion can be overcome only by another aversion or desire."

"What if someone threatens me with death? Does he not compel me then?"

It's not the threat of death that compels you but your own judgment that it is better to do something else than die. Your values compelled you and therefore you acted according to your will. If God had made it possible for his own fragment (that is us) to be hindered or compelled by anyone including himself, then he wouldn't be God, looking after us the way he has been.

The diviner says, "That's what I see inscribed in the sacrifice. This is God's signal to you: If you want, you are free. If you want, you will blame no one, you will accuse no one – if you want, everything will happen according to your plan, as well as God's." That's why we go to a diviner and a philosopher. Not to admire the interpreter, but to admire the interpretation.

Think about this

If you want, you are free. If you want, you will blame no one, you will accuse no one – if you want, everything will happen according to your plan. Discourses I.17.28. Epictetus [RD]

Why You Shouldn't Give in to Anger

Key ideas of this discourse

1. *The evidence of God's work is everywhere. You can see it even in insignificant things.*
2. *Instead of giving thanks for the gifts we have received, we keep complaining.*
3. *Let's constantly give thanks for the gifts we have received.*
4. *All our actions spring from a sole source. We do what appears to us to be right. We don't do what appears to us as wrong. When we are not sure, we suspend our judgment.*
5. *People who are antisocial such as thieves and adulterers, then, need our pity not our hatred. They were only doing what appeared to them to be right.*
6. *We get angry because we value external things. When we lose them, we get upset.*
7. *If we don't value external things, we won't get upset or angry.*

8. *We need to train ourselves not to value external things by starting with trivial things and moving on to bigger things.*

9. *Eventually, we need to test ourselves under different conditions to make sure that we don't value external things anymore.*

Feeling is the source of all actions

If what philosophers say is true, then all our actions arise from a lone source – feeling.

- when we agree with something, it is because we feel it must be so;
- when we disagree with something, it is because we feel it is not so; and
- when we suspend judgement, it is because we feel it is uncertain.

When we have an impulse to do a thing, it is because we feel it is to our advantage. It is impossible to consider something is to our advantage and do something else. Or, consider something right and have an urge to do something else. If all this is true, why should we be angry with anyone?

Antisocial people are misguided

"But there are thieves and robbers."

"What do you mean by 'thieves and robbers?' They are simply confused about what is good and what is bad. Should we then be angry with them or pity them? If you show them where they have gone wrong, they will reform. But if they don't see it, they will continue to rely on their opinion to guide them."

"Shouldn't we do away with thieves and adulterers?"

"By no means. Try putting your question this way: 'Shouldn't we get rid of people deceived in things that are most important?' You will realize how inhumane your position is. They are blind, not in vision that distinguishes black from white, but in the moral capacity that distinguishes good from bad. So, it is like saying 'Shouldn't we execute this blind man or deaf man?'"

People suffer greatest harm when they lose their greatest asset. Moral capacity is the greatest asset of all. So, if some people lose their moral capacity, why add anger to their greatest loss? If you are affected by them, show them pity, not hatred. Don't be too ready to hate and take offence. Why use common curses like, "Away with those abominable idiots," and the like? Let them be. Since when have you become so smart as to go around correcting other people's mistakes as though they are just fools?

We get angry because we value external things

Why then are we angry? Because we admire the things others take from us. Don't attach too high a value to your clothes and you won't get angry with the thief who steals them. Don't place too high a value on your spouse's attractiveness and you won't be angry with the adulterer. Remember that the thief and the adulterer cannot take what's yours, only what is common property, not under your control. If you give up ownership of things that are not yours, who will you be angry with then? If you value material things, direct your anger at yourself and not at the thief or adulterer.

Look at it this way. You have beautiful clothes, but your neighbor doesn't. You open your window to give them an airing. You neighbor does not know where human good truly lies and assumes it lies in good clothes. You think so too. Isn't it certain then that he is going to come along and steal them? When you display and gobble down food all by yourself, aren't you asking starving people to snatch it away from you? Don't provoke them. Don't have a window and don't air your clothes.

You cannot lose what you don't own

Something like this happened to me the other day. I had an iron lamp which I keep by my household shrine. I heard a noise from the window, ran down, and found it stolen. I reasoned that the thief had an irresistible impulse to steal it. I said to myself, "Tomorrow get a cheaper, earthenware lamp. You can only lose what you have."

"I lost my clothes."

"Yes, because you had clothes."

"I have a pain in the head."

"Did you expect to have a pain in the horns? Loss and sorrow are possible only with respect to what you own."

"But the tyrant will chain me."

"What will he chain? Your leg."

"He will cut it off."

"What will he cut off? Your head."

You have the power to choose

What he will never be able to cut off is your power to choose. This is the reason behind the ancient advice, "Know yourself."

We should discipline ourselves in trivial things, then move on to things of greater value. When you have a headache or earache, practice not cursing. If you complain, don't do it with your whole being. If your helper does not bring a bandage quickly, don't pull a face and say, "Everyone hates me!" Who wouldn't hate such a person?

From now on, place your faith in these principles. Walk upright and free. Don't trust the strength of your body as an athlete does. Don't just rely on your physical strength as a donkey does.

How to be invincible

You are invincible if nothing outside your will disturbs you.

Consider different possibilities as in the case of an athlete who won the first round.

- How will he do in the next one?
- How will he do if it is unbearably hot?
- How will he do at the Olympics?

Likewise, in the present instance. You offered him money, but he treated it with contempt. But,

- What if it is pretty girl whom he meets in the dark?
- What if it is a touch of glory?
- What if it is a bit of abuse or praise?
- What if it is death?

Can he handle all these things? And when it's hot, what if he's drunk? Or delirious or dreaming? If he can come through under all these challenges – then I would call him an invincible athlete.

Think about this

You are invincible if nothing outside your will can disconcert you. Discourses I.18.21. Epictetus [RD]

The Way to Act When You Meet the Powerful

Key ideas of this discourse

1. *Power, whether real or imaginary, makes people arrogant.*

2. *We are not frightened by what others might do to us; we are frightened by our thoughts about what might happen.*

3. *It is not antisocial to be self-interested. It is common to all beings.*

4. *We become subservient to others when we value external things.*

Power makes peoples arrogant

Uneducated people, if they have a real or imaginary advantage over others, will grow arrogant. A powerful person, for example, will say.

"I am very powerful."

"What can you do for me then? I want my desires unrestricted. Can you give me that?"

How can you? Have you achieved it for yourself? What else can you offer me? I want to avoid only those things I would like to avoid. Can you give me that? Have you achieved it for yourself? I always want to get what I want. Can you give that? When you are on a ship, you trust the pilot's expertise, not your own; when you are on a carriage, you trust the driver's skill. It is no different with other things. So, what does your superiority amount to?

"Everybody pays attention me."

"Well, I pay attention to my plate, wash it and wipe it. I pay attention to my oil flask – I drive a nail in the wall to hang it. Do these things make them better than me? No, it just means that they are of some use to me."

I look after my donkey too. I wash its feet and clean him down. Everyone looks after themselves and looks to you as they look to their donkey. Who respects you as a human being and wants to be like you, as if you were Socrates?

"But I can harm you."

"Oh, I forgot. I should watch out for you like I would for some virus or infection and erect an altar for you."

It's our thoughts that frighten us

What scares most people and keeps them frightened? It can't be the tyrant and the bodyguards. What nature has made free cannot be restrained by anything except by nature itself. A person's own thoughts can frighten her. If a tyrant threatens to chain our leg, whoever holds their leg in high regard will beg for mercy. A person who cares more for his character will say, "Go ahead and chain it, if you like."

"You don't care?"

"No, not in the least."

"Wait, I will show you who's in charge."

"How do you propose to do that? God has made me free and he is not going to allow his son to be enslaved. You are a master of my corpse and you are welcome to that."

"Do you mean to say that you will pay me no attention when you come across me?"

"No, I'd rather look after myself. If you insist, I will admit that I give you the same attention I give my dishes."

Self-interest is a common instinct and not antisocial

It is not us just being selfish. It is the way it is. Everything we do is done for our own ends. The sun moves across the sky for its own purpose. Even God acts on his own aims. But, while achieving his aims, God's actions benefit the world, so we respect Him as the giver of these benefits. He made rational beings the same way. Humans cannot achieve their personal goals without, at the same time, providing for the community, contributing to the common benefit. Finally, it is not antisocial to do everything for one's own sake. In any case, what do you expect? That we should not concern ourselves with our welfare? Then how do you explain the fact all living beings are driven by the same instinct of self-interest?

We grovel when we value things not under our control

When people hold absurd opinions about things not in their control, taking them to be good and bad, they will of course grovel before powerful people. Not only before the powerful but their flunkeys too!

Tell me, how does someone become wise when he is made a bathroom attendant by the emperor? Why do we suddenly say that 'Felicio [a common name for a slave/freedman] made such wise comments'? I hope he is kicked out of his position, so I can see you change your mind and consider him a fool again.

Epaphroditus [Epictetus' owner when he was a slave] once sold a slave because he was useless. The slave, who was a shoemaker, was bought by a member of Caesar's household. So, he became a shoemaker to the emperor. If only you had seen the way Epaphroditus honored him!

"How is my friend Felicio today?"

If someone asked us "Where is your master?" he was told, "He is in conference with Felicio."

Hadn't he sold him off because he was useless? How did he become so wise suddenly? Well, that's what happens when we value what is not under our control.

Someone is promoted. All who meet him congratulate him. They kiss his eyes and cheeks, even hands. At home, lights are lit in his honor. He climbs up the Capitol and offers a sacrifice of thanks. I ask you, who has ever offered thanks for the right desires or for impulses in agreement with nature? It seems that we only thank God for what we believe to be the good things in life.

A man asked me today about accepting an important public office, the priesthood of Augustus. I told him not to accept.

"You will incur a lot of expense for little return."

"But the clerk will add my name to a public contract."

"OK, you attend the signing ceremonies now. What happens when you die?"

"My name will survive me."

"Carve it in stone, and it will survive equally well. Outside this city, no one will remember this."

"But I get to wear a crown of gold."

"If your heart is set on a crown, make one out of roses. You will look prettier in that."

Think about this

It is not antisocial to be constantly acting in one's own self-interest. Discourses I.19.15. Epictetus [RD]

[God made it so that] Human beings are incapable of attaining any of their private ends without at the same time providing for the common good.

When people hold absurd opinions about things that lie outside the sphere of choice, regarding them good or evil, it is quite inevitable that they pay court to tyrants. Discourses I.19.16. Epictetus [CH/RH]

Use Reason to Evaluate Impressions

Key ideas of this discourse

1. *Reason is the supreme faculty because it can examine all other faculties as well as itself.*
2. *We should not accept untested impressions. Yet, we accept first impressions as being true and are unconcerned about good and evil.*
3. *The essential teaching is simple: "Follow God and distinguish impressions correctly." Yet, clearly distinguishing impressions requires long study and effort. But it is well worth it, because this is the greatest art of all.*

Arts and faculties cannot examine themselves

Take the art of shoemaking. It concerns itself with leather, but leather is not shoe-making. Therefore, shoe-making does not examine itself. Again, grammar is applied to written words.

But grammar itself is not written words. Therefore, grammar does not examine itself. It is so with every art and faculty. Every art focuses on some subject and can only examine things that are of the same nature as the faculty but not things of a different nature.

Nature has given us reason, so we can examine all faculties

"Why has nature given us the faculty of reason?"

"To make proper use of impressions."

"What is reason itself?"

"It is a collection of various impressions. Nature made reason capable of examining itself."

"To examine what? Why are we given this wisdom?"

"To examine what is good, what is bad, and what is neither. So, what is wisdom?"

"A good thing."

"And foolishness?"

"A bad thing."

"You see then that wisdom can examine itself and its opposite."

Do not accept untested impressions

For that reason, our most important job is to test our impressions and accept only those that pass the test. We believe our interests are affected by money. So, we have developed the art of assaying if the coins are counterfeit: by sight, touch, smell, and hearing. The assayer drops a silver coin and listens closely to its ring. Not once but many times. By frequent attention to it, he has become quite a musician. Similarly, whenever we believe it makes a difference, whether we get something right or wrong, we must play close attention and distinguish those things that might mislead us.

But when it comes to our poor ruling faculty, we yawn and go back to sleep, accepting every impression that comes our way. It does not occur to us that this will affect us in any way.

Do you want to know how unconcerned you are about what is good and bad and how eager you are about things that are indifferent? Compare your attitude towards physical blindness with blind judgements. You will see that you are far from having the feelings that you should have in relation to good and evil.

"But this requires long preparation, much effort, and study."

"So what? Do you expect to master the greatest of arts with little study?"

Essentials are simple, understanding them is not

Yet, the most essential teachings of philosophers are succinct. Read [Stoic philosopher] Zeno's works and you will see. How long does it take to say, "Follow God and the essence of good consists in the correct use of impressions"? Then if you ask, "What is God?", "What is an impression?", "What is the nature of the individual in the universe?" the discussion becomes lengthy. If Epicurus should come along and say that goodness must reside in our flesh, the discussion grows longer still.

You need to learn all about our principal part, our substantial nature, and our essential nature. It is unlikely the good of the snail lie in its shell. Why should it in the case of human beings? [So, we challenge Epicurus.]

"What do you yourself have that is superior to that, Epicurus? What is there within you that deliberates, examines everything, and decides that flesh is the principal part? Why do you light your lamp and labor for us, writing so many books? That we may not be ignorant of the truth? Who are we? What are we to you?"

So, the argument becomes long.

Think about this

The most important task of a philosopher, and his first task, is to test out impressions and distinguish between them, and not to accept any impression unless it has been duly tested. Discourses I.20.7. Epictetus [RD]

Don't Seek Admiration, be Well-Grounded

Key idea of this discourse

It is the mark of a well-grounded person not to look for outside approval.

If you are well-grounded in life, you don't need to look beyond it

"What is it you want, my friend?"

"I am happy if my desires and aversions are in line with nature. And, if I exercise impulse to act or not to act and practice purpose, design, and assent the same way."

"Then why do you walk around as though you have swallowed a spit?"

"I want everyone I meet to admire me and, as they follow after me, say, "What a great philosopher!""

"Who are these people that you want to be admired by? Aren't they the same ones whom you used to call crazy? Well, then, do you want to be admired by madmen?"

Think about this

When someone is properly grounded in life, they shouldn't have to look outside themselves for approval. Discourses I.21.1. Epictetus [RD]

We Are in Conflict Because We Value Externals

Key ideas of this discourse

1. *We all share the same preconceptions about good and evil.*
2. *However, we get into conflict with each other because we don't agree on how they apply to a given situation.*
3. *We need to understand what is in our power and what is not. Good and evil arise from what is under our power, not from externals.*
4. *Placing value on externals result in contradiction and conflict.*

We all agree on basic principles

There are some preconceptions on which we all agree. After all, who does not think that good is beneficial, choice is desirable, and we should pursue them? Who does not assume that justice is fair and appropriate?

Our conflicts arise in the application of principles

Then why do we have conflicts? Conflicts arise because of the way we apply our preconceived ideas differently to individual cases. The same person may be judged as brave by one but as reckless by another. This is how conflict arises. It is the source of differences among the Jews, Syrians, Egyptians, and Romans. They agree that what is holy is to be preferred and pursued. But they argue about what is holy: for example, to eat or not to eat pork. This is how Agamemnon and Achilles got into conflict.

"What do you say, Agamemnon? Shouldn't we do what is right and proper?"

"Yes, of course."

"What do you say, Achilles? Do you agree?

"Yes, more than anything else."

"Go ahead and apply your principles."

The conflict begins. Agamemnon says, "I shouldn't have to return to Chryseis to her father."

Achilles says, "You should."

Clearly, one of them is wrong in the way he applied his principles in this case.

Then Agamemnon says, "Fine, if I give Chryseis back, then I should get one of your prizes."

"I hope it is not the woman I love."

"Yes, it is."

"Why should I lose my prize, of all people?"

This is how conflicts begin.

Placing value on externals results in contradictions

To be properly educated means learning to apply our natural preconceptions to events, according to nature – distinguishing what is in our power and what is not in our power. In our power are choice and all actions that arise out of our choice. Not in our power are our body, body parts, property, parents, siblings, children, country, or friends.

"Where does good come from then?"

"From things in our power."

"It follows then that neither health nor fitness are good; nor our children, parents, or country."

"This view is not going to win you many converts."

"All right then. Let's call external things such as health 'good' and see what happens. Suppose a person suffers harm and fails to obtain good things. Could such a person still be happy?"

"No, it is not possible."

"Can he live with his neighbors in the same way he had lived in the past?"

"How is it possible? They have their own self-interest."

"If it is in my own self-interest to own land, it is in my interest to rob it from my neighbors. If it is in my interest to own a coat, it is in my interest to steal it from the baths."

How can this be in line with my duty to God? Because, if I am harmed and meet with misfortune, I start to wonder whether he pays any attention to me. If he won't help me, and wishes me to be in this condition, what is he to me? So, I begin to hate him. I wonder whether the temples and statues we build for him are more like things intended to placate evil demons. How can he be the "Savior," "Rain-bringer," or "Fruit-bringer"? All this follows from identifying the "good" with externals. What are we to do? That is the inquiry to be made by the person who philosophizes and thinks deep.

"I do not see what is good and evil. Am I crazy?"

"Yes."

"But if I place 'The good' in the realm of my choice, I might be ridiculed. Some grey-haired old man with gold rings on his fingers will come along and say, 'Learning philosophy is all right up to a point, but don't get carried away. This is ridiculous. Philosophers can teach you logic, but you know how to behave better than they do.'"

If I know how to behave as he says, then why does he find fault with me? What can I say to this fool? If I don't answer, he gets angry. So, I answer this way:

"Bear with me as you would with someone in love. I can't help myself. I am crazy."

Think about this

What does it mean to be getting an education? It means learning to apply natural preconceptions to events as nature prescribes and distinguishing what is in our power from what is not. Discourses I.22.9. Epictetus [RD]

External Things Are of No Value

Key ideas of this discourse

1. *Epicurus discourages people from bringing up children or participating in politics. This is because he has identified our good with external things.*
2. *We are social beings. Affection between parents and children is natural. So is our involvement in the political process.*
3. *It does not make sense for human beings, who are naturally social, to live like unsocial flies.*

Epicurus' mistake: Placing value on external things

Even Epicurus realizes that, by nature, we are social beings. But once he has placed our good in what is merely our shell, he cannot say anything that is not in line with it. He further insists – rightly so – that we should not accept or respect anything that is not part of what is good.

Questions for Epicurus

- How can we be social beings if we don't have natural affection for our children?
- Why do you, Epicurus, discourage a wise man from bringing up children?
- Why are you afraid that, upon their arrival, a wise man will become unhappy?
- Are you anxious on behalf of your house-slave? A mouse? What is it to you?

We are social beings

Epicurus knows that, once a child is born, it is impossible for us not to love and care for it. That's why he also says that a wise man will not take part in politics either. He knows political affairs involve personal connections. Well, if you want to live like flies among humans, what stops you?

Not even a sheep or wolf deserts its offspring

He knows all this and yet has the audacity to say, "Let's not bring up children." Not even a sheep or wolf deserts its offspring; should a human being?

What do you want? To be as foolish as sheep or as savage as wolves, neither of them abandon its young? Tell me, who would take your advice if they saw their little child fallen on the floor and crying? Personally, I think that your parents, even if they had known you were going to say such things, would not have gotten rid of you.

Think about this

[We] must not respect or approve anything that does not share in the nature of what is good. Discourses I.23.2. Epictetus [RD]

Difficult Times Reveal What a Person is Made Of

Key ideas of this discourse

1. *Think of difficulties as opportunities for training.*
2. *Understand that external things are nothing to us.*
3. *Don't fear others. You don't have to, if you don't lay claim on externals.*
4. *Don't envy others. Outwardly successful people can be tragic figures.*
5. *If you don't want to play the game quit. Stay or leave, don't complain.*

Difficulties are training opportunities

It is difficulties that show what a person is made of. So, when you face some difficulty, think of yourself as a wrestler. God, as your trainer, has matched you with a tough young opponent. But why? To turn you into Olympic-class material. This cannot be done without sweat. The way I see it, no one's difficulties ever gave him a better test than yours – if you are willing to make use of them the way a wrestler makes use of well-conditioned opponent.

Understand that externals are nothing to us

We are now sending you to Rome as a spy. But we don't want a coward for a spy – someone who is quick to turn back at the first noise or a glimpse of a shadow, completely frightened and announce, "The enemy is practically among us."

When you return, if you tell us, "Things are dreadful in Rome. Death, exile, poverty, and spies are everywhere. Run you people, the enemy is already among us!" then we will tell you,

"Get lost. And keep your forecasts to yourself. Our only mistake was to send out such a spy."

We had sent Diogenes as a spy and he came back with a vastly different report. He said, "Death is no evil, because it is not dishonorable. Reputation is the empty noise of fools." He brought great news to remove pain, pleasure, and poverty. He preferred little clothing to purple robes, bare ground to a soft bed. And to prove his claims he produced his courage, tranquility, and freedom as well as his tough, radiant body.

He said, "There are no enemies nearby! All is profound peace."

"How so, Diogenes?"

"Look at me. Am I wounded, disabled, or running away from anyone?

Don't envy others

That's how a spy should be. Instead, you bring us all random things. Go back and examine things more closely, setting aside your cowardice.

"What should I do then?"

"What do you do when you leave a ship? Do you take the rudder and oars with you? No, you leave with your own luggage, oil-flask, and wallet. If you remember what belongs to you, you won't lay claim to what belongs to others."

The emperor says, "Take off your consul's robe."

"Then I will wear a plain toga."

"Take off that too."

"Fine, I will go naked."

"I still envy your calm."

"Take my whole body then. Take it all."

Is there any reason to fear anyone, if I am ready give up my body?

You protest, "But so-and-so will not leave his estate to me. What then?" Did you forget that none of it is yours? How then do you call it your own? Do you call the hotel bed yours? If the hotel-owner dies and leaves the beds to you, you will have it. If she leaves it to someone else, he will have it. You will have to find another bed or sleep on the floor. Do so with courage, and snore away.

Remember, tragedies take place among the rich and among kings and tyrants. No poor man fills a tragic role except as a member of the chorus. Kings start off in prosperity: "Decorate the palace with festive garlands." But about the third or fourth act, "O Cithaeron, why did you receive me?" [Cithaeron was the mountain on which the infant Oedipus was left to die.] Fool, where are your crowns? Where is your diadem? Even your guards can't help you now. So, remember, when you meet someone like this, you are in the presence of a tragic figure, not an actor but Oedipus himself.

"But he is so blessed to walk around with an entourage."

"Join a crowd. You too will have an entourage."

Stay or leave, but quit complaining

So, remember that the door is open. Don't be more cowardly than children who say, when they are tired of the game, "I will play no more."

When you feel weary of the game, say "I will play no more" and depart. If you stay, quit complaining.

Think about this

It is difficulties that show what men are. Discourses I.24.1. Epictetus [WO]

Placing Value on Externals Creates Conflicts

Key ideas of this discourse

1. *We are anxious because we don't accept that good and evil arise out of our moral choices, not by external things.*
2. *No one can take away what belongs to us.*
3. *We create our own problems by choosing to attach value to external things.*
4. *We always have the option of choosing what happens, as it happens.*

You will not be anxious once you understand that good and evil are your choices

If what we have been discussing so far is true and we are not being stupid or pretending to agree, then we know:

- Good and evil arise out of the choices we make; and
- All else is nothing to us.

Why are we still anxious? No one has power over things that deeply concern us. What they control, we don't care about. What is there left to worry about?

"I still need specific instructions."

"What instructions do you want me to give? Has not God already given you the rules?"

Has he not given you what is your own, free from restraint or hindrance? And that what is not your own is subject to both? What other commandments did you arrive with when you came here?

- Protect what is yours at all costs
- Don't crave for things that belong to another
- Your good faith and sense of shame are your own

No one can take away what belongs to you

Who can take these away from you? Who can stop you from making use of these except you? Only when you go after what is not yours, you lose what is yours. Why do you need further instructions from me? Am I greater than God and to be trusted more? Follow his commandments and you won't need others. As proof that he has delivered them to you, bring me your preconceptions, what you have heard from philosophers, what you have said to yourself, and what you have practiced.

"How long should I observe these rules before breaking up the game?"

"As long as the game remains a pleasure. At the Saturnalia game, a king is chosen by lot. He orders others: 'You drink!' 'You sing!' 'You go!' 'You come!' I obey because I don't want to be the one to break up the game."

"Suppose the king asks you to imagine that you are unhappy."

"I don't suppose that, but I refuse. Who is going to force me? Suppose now we agree to play Agamemnon and Achilles. If the person playing Agamemnon says to me, 'Go get Breisis away from Achilles.' I go. 'Come.' I come."

Use hypothetical scenarios to model your behavior

We should use hypothetical arguments as models for how to behave in life.

"Let it be night."

"OK."

"Is it day now?"

"No, because that is not consistent with the hypothesis I agreed to."

The same applies here.

"Suppose you have come upon hard times."

"All right."

"Are you unfortunate and unhappy then?"

"Yes."

"Now you are really in a bad way."

"No, because that is not consistent with the hypothesis I agreed to. Besides, there is another [here Epictetus referring to God - W.A. Oldfather] who forbids me to think so."

"How long should we follow the rules of the game?"

"As long as it serves your turn. As long as it is congenial."

Miserable and inflexible people will say, "I can't eat at this man's table if it means listening to his war stories again: 'I told you my friend, how I scrambled up the hill; I will start again with the siege.'"

But another person might say, "For me what matters is the meal; let him rattle on as much as likes."

It is for you to compare the value of things. But do not do anything resentfully, as if someone forced it upon you.

You always have options

Is there a smoke in the house? If it is not suffocating, stay. If it is, get out. Always remember: the door is open.

"Don't live in Nicopolis."

"I won't live there."

"Don't live in Athens."

"Okay, I won't live in Athens either."

"Live on Gyara."

But, for me, living on Gyara is like living in a smoky house. So, I go to the one place no one can stop me from going. A place where everyone is welcome. When I remove all my clothing including my skin, then no one can hold me any longer. Thus, Demetrius challenged Nero: "You threaten me with death, but nature threatens you with it."

If I place value on my body, I make a slave of myself; if I place a value on my property, again I make a slave of myself because I have shown how I may be taken. When a snake pulls its head back, I say "Hit the part it is protecting." Similarly, whatever you are seen to protect will become the target for your enemy. Remember this, and you will fear or flatter no one.

"But I want to sit along in the senators' gallery."

"Don't you see, you are closing yourself in. You are treading on your own toes."

"How else can I get a proper view of the stage?"

"Don't strive for a view and you won't be crowded. What is the problem? Or wait until the show is over and you can sit in a senator's seat and sun yourself at leisure."

We create our own problems

It is generally true that we crush ourselves and create problems for ourselves. That is, our opinions do. For example, what does it mean to be insulted? Stand by a stone and insult it, what response will you get? Likewise, if you listen like a stone, what would the abuser gain by his abuse? However, if you have some weakness, then he has an advantage over you.

"Strip him!"

"What do you mean 'Strip him? Take my clothes?'"

"I have insulted you."

"Much good may do it to you."

That's what Socrates practiced and that's why he always had the same expression on his face. But it looks like we would practice anything other than how to remain unrestrained and free.

"Philosophers talk in paradoxes."

What about other arts? What is more paradoxical than cutting into a person's eyes to make him see? If you say this to someone who has no knowledge of medicine, would he not laugh at your face? Why are you surprised then if many truths appear paradoxical to the ignorant?

Think about this

Man's good and man's evil lies in moral choice, and all other things are nothing to us. Discourses I.25.1. Epictetus [WO]

The Law of Life: Live in Accordance with Nature

Key ideas of this discourse

1. *Live in accordance with nature.*
2. *Become aware of this governing principle.*
3. *Start with ideas that are easy to understand and then go on to more difficult ones.*

We must do what follows from nature

Epictetus saw someone reading out hypothetical arguments.

He said "True, there is a law governing hypothesis – we must admit what follows from the hypothesis." Then he continued, "Far more important is the law of life – we must do what follows from nature. If we desire to obey nature in every area and on every occasion, then we should neither miss noticing what nature expects of us nor accept anything that conflicts with it."

Start with what is easy to understand

So, philosophers start with theory that is easier to understand, leaving more difficult subjects for later. When we study theory, there is nothing to challenge what we are being taught; but in real life many things clamor for our attention. It is silly to argue otherwise because it is not easy to begin with what is more difficult.

This is the right defense to use with parents who are displeased with their children studying philosophy.

"I am sure you are right, Dad. My judgment is poor, and I don't know how I should go about it. But if it can neither be taught nor be learned, then why blame me? But if it can be taught, please teach it to me yourself. Or, let me learn from someone who claims to understand it. Besides, do you believe I would voluntarily choose evil and miss the good? I hope not! Why then do I go wrong if not for my ignorance? Do you not then want me to get rid of my ignorance? When did anger ever teach anyone how to play music or how to pilot a ship? Do you expect your anger to teach me the art of living?"

You can use these arguments only if your motives have those intentions. But if a person goes to philosophers and studies these things to impress others with his knowledge at a dinner party, he'd be satisfied to gain the respect of a senator seated next to him.

We can find great resources in Rome. The wealth we find here in Nicolpolis, by comparison, is mere child's play. It is easy to follow your principles here because there aren't many temptations. It is more difficult to master your impressions in Rome because several temptations compete for your attention there. I once saw a man who wept and embraced the knees of Epaphroditus (my former master in Rome) saying that he was down to his last million. What did Epaphroditus do? Laugh at him, as you are doing now? No! He said in an astonished tone: "Poor fellow. How did you manage to keep silent all these days? How did you endure it?"

Once Epictetus corrected someone reading the hypothetical arguments. The person who set him reading began ridiculing him to which Epictetus replied: "You are ridiculing yourself. You did not prepare the student, so he could understand these arguments and you did not care to find out if he could understand these arguments. You simply used him as a reader. If a mind can't follow the conclusion of a complex argument, how can you assume such a mind is capable of assigning praise or blame and forming judgments about things being good or bad? If such a person talks ill of someone, will the other person care? If he praises someone, will that someone jump for joy, when the person in question cannot even follow logic in simple matters?"

Know your mental state regarding the governing principle

So, if one wants to be a philosopher, one should first become aware of one's governing principle. When a person knows it is in a weak state, he will refrain from tackling difficult matters. The way it is now though, some people who cannot work though a leaflet will try to devour a whole treatise. The result? They get sick or suffer indigestion.

Worse things follow. They should first find out what they are capable of. In matters of theory, it is easy to refute someone who is ignorant. But, in the affairs of life, no one offers himself to be examined. We resent being examined as well. Yet Socrates used to say that the unexamined life is not worth living.

Think about this

[The] law of life ... we must do what nature demands. Discourses I.26.2. Epictetus [WO]

Ways to Deal with External Impressions

Key ideas of this discourse

1. *External impressions can be deceptive. The duty of an educated person is to judge all impressions correctly.*
2. *Choose the right resource for the right job. To combat a habit, choose a contrary habit.*
3. *We cannot escape death, but we can escape the fear of it.*
4. *There is no point in trying to convince the sceptics, if you have better things to do with your time.*

Impressions come to us in four ways

There are four types of external impressions
1. Things are, and they appear to be
2. Things are not and do not appear to be
3. Thing are, but do not appear to be
4. Things are not, but appear to be

An educated person should judge impressions correctly in all these cases.

Find the right remedy for the right problem

If we find it difficult to judge impressions, we need to use the right kind of resources to find a solution.

If the sceptics (who, like Academics and Pyrrhonists, argue that we can know nothing for certain) bother us with their sophisms, let us seek remedy for that.

If we are concerned about the plausibility of things – when things appear good when they are not – let us seek a corrective for that.

If we are troubled by our habits, let's find a remedy for that. What aid can we find against habit? The contrary habit.

Ignorant people commonly say, "He died. Poor man. His father died, his mother too. He died before his time, somewhere abroad." Listen to all that but distance yourself from such statements.

Check each habit with a contrary habit. If sophistry, then the art of reasoning. Against false impressions, we should have clear preconceptions polished and ready for use.

Why death is no evil

When death appears an evil to you, remember that it is our duty to avoid evil. But we can't avoid death, because it is a necessity. How can I get away from it? Where will I go? If you are a son of God you can say in a noble manner, "I will go on this journey to win glory for myself or give another the opportunity to gain it. If I cannot win glory, I will not grudge giving the opportunity to another."

Granted that such declarations are beyond us, can't we at least accept the alternative (that death is no evil) that is within our power?

"Where can I go to escape death? Show me the country, give me the names of those who are safe from death and give me a magic charm against it. If I have none of these, what do you expect me to do?"

"I cannot escape death. Can't I escape the fear of it? Or do I have to die moaning and groaning too?"

We are frustrated when our wishes are not fulfilled. So, if I can shape external conditions to suit my wishes, I will do so; if I cannot, I stand ready to tear out the eyes of anyone who stands in my way. If you are distressed, don't spend your time trying to convince the sceptics.

People, by nature, can endure neither being deprived of the good nor meeting up with evil. So, when I can't change things or tear out the eyes of anyone who stands in my way, I sit and groan, and blame God. What is he to me, if doesn't look after me?

"You are being impious."

"What punishment would make my situation any worse? Surely, if piety is incompatible with self-interest, no one will be pious. Aren't you convinced?"

No time for sceptics

Let a sceptic come forward to oppose us. I have neither time for this nor can I advocate commonly-held beliefs. If I have a property dispute, I would call a lawyer to help me. What will help me here? Someone who is appropriate. If you ask me if the way I see something involves my entire body or only a part of it, I may not be able to answer, because both alternatives seem problematic to me. But I am positive that you and I are not the same person.

"How do you know that?"

"When I want to swallow something, I don't carry it to your mouth but my own. If I want bread, I don't pick up a broom, but go directly to the loaf as if it were a target. Do you sceptics, who deny the evidence of all senses, act any differently? Which of you went to a mill when you needed a bath?"

"Well, should we not then defend convention and watch out for any attacks on it?"

"Sure, if you have the time for it. But the broken-hearted person who is trembling and upset needs to spend her time differently, though."

Think about this

What aid, then, is it possible to discover against habit? The contrary habit. Discourses I.27.4 Epictetus [CG/RH]

Don't Be Angry with Others

Key ideas of this discourse

1. *We accept things to be true or false because they appear so to us.*

2. *Even when people act in destructive ways, it is because they have accepted their impressions as true, without examining them.*

3. *We should not be angry with others, because they are doing what they believe to be right.*

4. *All human misery and tragedies are the result of accepting sense-impressions to be true.*

5. *What counts for good and bad comes from our actions, not from externals.*

6. *Therefore, we should examine our impressions carefully before accepting them. This is what distinguishes humans from animals.*

We accept things as true, if they appear to be so

"Why do we accept something to be true?"

"Because it appears so to us. If something appears to us to be false, it would be impossible for us to accept it."

"Why?"

"Because this is the nature of our mind: Accept what is true, reject what is false, and suspend judgment on uncertain things."

"Prove it."

"Think of this as night."

"That's impossible. (It's day now.)"

"Put aside the impression that it is day."

"That's impossible."

"Think that there are/are not even number of stars."

"Impossible again."

When people act on mistaken beliefs, we should not be angry with them

So, if someone agrees to what is false, we can be sure that she doesn't do so willingly (as Plato says, our mind is deprived of truth against its will), but it appears so to that person.

"In terms of action, do we have anything corresponding to true or false perceptions: What is our duty and what is not, what is beneficial and what is not, what is appropriate and what is not and so on?"

"A person cannot think of something to be of benefit to her and yet not choose it. Agreed?"

"But what about Medea who said, 'I know what I intend to do is evil; but my sober thoughts are overpowered by my passion.' "

"In her case, it is no different. She believed that gratifying her anger by taking revenge on her husband was more beneficial than saving her children."

"But she's wrong."

"Show her clearly where she went wrong, and she won't do it. But if you don't show it, what else has she got to go by, except what seems right to her?"

"Nothing."

"Why are you angry with her then? Poor woman, she is so confused about what is most important that, instead of being a human being, she has become a snake. Pity her instead."

We take pity on the blind and lame. Why don't we pity those who are blind and lame in their ruling faculty? Remember that our actions are the result of our impressions, which can be right or wrong. If right, you are innocent and if you are wrong, you pay the penalty. It is not as though if you go astray, someone else will pay the penalty. If you keep this in mind, you will not be angry or upset with anyone, won't insult, criticize, hate, or be offended by anyone.

"So, in your view, are great and dreadful deeds the result of sense-impressions?"

"Yes. The result of that and only that."

Tragedies are the result of mistaken impressions

The *Iliad* is nothing but a sense impression and the poet's interpretation of it. An impression made Paris abduct Menelaus' wife and an impression made Helen follow him. If an impression had caused Menelaus to think that he was better off without her, then not only the *Iliad* would have been lost, but the *Odyssey* as well.

"Are you then saying that such momentous events depend on such a small cause?"

"Which of these events do you call great: Wars and factions, deaths of many men, destruction of cities? What is great about that? Nothing. What about slaughtering many oxen, sheep, burning a lot of storks' and swallows' nests?"

"Can you really compare the two?"

"They are remarkably similar. In one case death happened to human beings and, in the other, to farm animals. People's houses were burnt in one case, storks' nests in the other. What is great or dreadful in all this? How is a house, merely a shelter, better than a stork's nest?"

"Are men and storks similar then?"

"There is a great similarity where the body is concerned. Only that in man's case his body lives in brick and mortar houses, while storks live in nests made of sticks and mud."

"So, there is no difference between a person and a stork?"

"Far from it. But not in these external things."

"In what ways do they differ, then?"

"Think about it. You will realize that humans differ in other respects: in their understanding of their actions, being sociable, trustworthy, honest, and intelligent and in learning from their mistakes."

"Where does good and evil come from then?"

"From things in which humans differ from animals. If you keep these qualities well protected, do not lose your honor, trustworthiness, or intelligence, then you are saved. But if you lose any of these qualities, or if they are overtaken by turbulence, then you are then lost."

All important things depend on this. Paris' tragedy was not that Greeks invaded Troy and killed his brothers. No, because no one falls because of the actions of others. What went on then was mere destruction of stork's nests. He fell when he lost his modesty, trustworthiness, respect for the laws of hospitality, and decency.

Similarly, Achilles' tragedy was not in the death of Patroclus. Not at all. It was when he gave in to anger weeping over an insignificant woman, forgetting he was not there for romance but to wage a war.

These are the ways in which human beings are defeated. This is the siege, the destruction of one's city, when a person's right judgments are torn down and destroyed.

"When women are held captive, children are enslaved, and men are slaughtered – are these things not evil?"

"How do you justify adding your opinion to these things? Do let me in on it too."

"No. You explain to me how these are not evils?"

Good and evil come from us, not from externals

Let's start with our standard and understand our preconceptions first. How people act in this regard is what amazes me. When we want to judge weights, we don't judge at random. When we want to judge when something is straight or crooked, we don't decide it at random. Whenever truth makes a difference to us on anything, we would not go for random judgements.

Yet when it comes to the first and foremost cause of good or bad conduct, happiness or adversity, and success or failure, we act impulsively and at random. We don't use any standard of measurement or scale. Some impression that appears right strikes us and we act on that basis.

Are we better than Agamemnon and Achilles? While they suffered the consequences of following their impressions, could we follow our impressions (without suffering the consequences)? Is there any tragedy that has a different source?

"How about Atreus of Euripides? The Oedipus of Sophocles? The Phoenix? Hippolytus?"

"All impressions."

"Who then pays no attention to the matter of impressions?"

"Let's see, what do we call those who follow every impression?"

"Mad."

"Do we act any differently?"

Think about this

What is the reason we assent to anything? The fact that it appears to us to be so. Discourses I.28.1. Epictetus [WO]

Be Steadfast in Your Practice

Key ideas of this discourse

1. *Good and evil come from our choices. If our judgement about externals is correct, our choice is good; if our judgement is distorted or crooked, then our choice is bad. Therefore, if you want something good, get it from yourself.*

2. *Someone who threatens you physically can only threaten your body. If you lose the fear of externals, including your body, there is nothing left to fear.*

3. *No one has control over what is yours, no matter how many opponents you face and no matter how powerful they are otherwise.*

4. *You can always give up your life when there is a good reason to do so but not for trivial reasons.*

5. *When you cannot change another person's mind, realize that the person is no more than a child.*

6. *When you face crises, see them as opportunities to practice what you have learned and use them so.*

7. *Do not be bothered when ignorant people judge you. Don't indulge in petty arguments.*

8. *No one is master over another. We are ruled by life and death, pleasure, and pain.*

9. *If you free yourself from our emotions, you will not have any troubles.*

10. *Don't preach to those who are not ready to understand.*

Good and evil do not come from externals

Good and evil come from our choices.

"What are external things then?"

"Externals are the means we use for good or evil."

"How do we find good?"

"We find good by not attaching value to externals which are just the means. If our judgement about externals is correct, our choice is good; if our judgement is distorted or crooked, then our choice is bad."

This is a God-given law: If you want something good, get it for yourself. But you say that you'd get it from someone else. I repeat, get it from yourself. If some tyrant threatens me, I say

"What are you threatening?"

"I will put you in chains."

"Oh, you are threatening my hands and feet."

"I will behead you."

"Oh, you are threatening my neck."

"I will throw you in prison."

"Now you are threatening my entire body. If you threaten me with exile, I will say the same."

It is not me who he is really threatening. No, not if I completely believe externals are nothing to me. But if I am afraid for any of it, then it is me he threatens. What is left there for me to fear? What does he have control over? Over things in my power? No one has control over those except me. Over things not in my power? I don't care about those.

No one has power over what is in your control

It is not about philosophers being disrespectful of authority. Not at all. You will not find any of us philosophers teaching disrespect for those who act within their proper authority. They can have all my body, my property, my reputation, and those that are about me. I challenge anyone to show that I encourage others to lay claim on those things.

"Yes, but I want to control your judgement too."

"Who gave you that power? How can you conquer another person's judgement?"

If the king says he will win with fear, then I would say he doesn't seem to understand that mind can only be conquered by itself, not by another. Nothing else can overcome the power of choice but itself. For that reason, the law of God, "Let the better always prevail over the worse," is excellent and just.

"But aren't ten people stronger than one person?"

"In what though? Only in things they are superior: such as restraining, killing, and dragging people away, taking their property."

"In what way are they worse then?"

"A person with correct judgement is superior to ten without correct judgment. Put them in the balance. The person with correct judgement would drag down the scales."

"Are you saying then that it was all right for Socrates to have suffered at the hands of Athenians?"

"Not Socrates, idiot. Say it as it really is. The poor body of Socrates was seized, dragged, and thrown into prison by stronger men. Someone gave his poor body hemlock and it died."

Your body is an external. Your judgements are not

Do you think all this is so unjust that you should blame God? Didn't Socrates have other resources to offset all this? What was the essence of the good for him? Do you want us to listen to you or to him when he said, "Anytus and Meleuts can kill me, but they cannot harm me. If it pleases the gods, so be it."

Show me a person who can get the better of someone with superior judgement. Try all you want, but you cannot, you can't even come close. This is the law of nature: "Let the better be always be superior to the worse."

Better where? Only one's area of expertise. One body is stronger than another body, many bodies are stronger than one, and a thief is stronger than those that are not thieves. That's how I came to lose my lamp – the thief was better at keeping awake than I. But he had a price to pay for the lamp: for its sake, he became a thief, lost his ability to be trusted, and became a brute. He thought it was a good bargain!

"It is easy for you to talk like that. But here I am grabbed by my collar and dragged down the streets. Then someone shouts at me: 'Hey philosopher, what good have your views done you? Look, you are being dragged off to prison and soon you may lose your life too.' Tell me, what *Introduction to Philosophy* could I have read that would have saved me from a situation like this? It is not that I have learned nothing. Philosophy taught me that I should be indifferent to things beyond my control. They are nothing to me."

"So, have you not benefited from knowing this? Why do you look for help from philosophy except in those areas it can help you?"

As I sit in prison I can think to myself that anyone who laughs at me is deaf to the real meaning of words. They cannot understand what they hear. Neither do they care to know what philosophers say or do. Let them be. I hear,

"Come out of prison."

"If you don't want me to be in prison any more, I will come out. If you do, I will go back again.'"

"How long will you keep this up?"

"As long as reason tells me that I need to be alive. When reason tells me otherwise, you can take my body and good health to you!"

We must not take our lives without reason

But we must not take our own life without reason, or because it has become feeble, or for some other trivial reason. It is contrary to the will of God. He needs such a world and creatures like us. If he gives the signal, as he did in the case of

Socrates, we must obey it as you would if it from your commander-in-chief.

"Should we tell this to all and sundry?"

"What would be the point? Is it not enough to convince ourselves of this?"

Be tolerant of those who cannot understand

If children come to us clapping their hands chanting, "Today is good Saturnalia," do we say, "There's no good in that?" No, we join them and clap our hands too. So, when you cannot change a person's mind, recognize that he is a child. Clap hands with him. If you cannot bring yourself to do that, just be silent.

Challenging times are opportunities to practice what you have learned

It is important to remember this so, when you face demanding situations, you will know it is time to show what you have learned. A good student just out of school would not look for easy problems to solve. An athlete would not like to be paired with someone with inferior ability. But when a crisis comes, we start groaning and want to keep on learning. Learn what? If you cannot demonstrate in practice what you learned, why learn it in the first place?

I guess some of you might be sitting here losing patience and thinking, "When will I face a challenge like the one he did? I am growing old here sitting in a corner while I could be winning at the Olympics. When will it be my time to face a similar challenge"' That's the attitude that all of you should develop.

There are gladiators in Rome who get frustrated when they are called up to fight and matched with an inferior opponent. They beg God and their supervisors to be allowed to fight. None of you here show such spirit. I would like to escape to Rome just to see my athlete in action; how he, at least, practices what he has learned.

"These are not the circumstances I want"

"It is not up to you to choose them. You are given a body, parents and brothers, a country, and a position in it. You come here expecting me to change these. You are not even aware of the assets you already have that will make it possible to cope with any situation you face."

You should instead say, "Tell me what to do, and I will practice it well." Instead you want to choose what problems I should set for you. You want to decide on the conclusions as well. A time will come, I suppose, when actors will think of their masks, high-heeled boots, and long robes as themselves. "Man, these things are your materials and you have a part to play. Say something so we'll know whether you are an actor or a buffoon – both have common costumes but not the same voice." If I take away the costume does the actor remain? He does, if he has the right voice.

No matter what life offers you, play your part well

So it is in life. "Take this job as a governor."

I take it and show how a properly educated person behaves.

"Take off your senator's robe and put on beggar's clothes. Come on the stage as that character."

So what? I still have the power to use my fine voice. "What role do you want me to play now?" As a witness called by God.

"Come on then, you earned the right to represent me as a witness. Is there anything good or bad outside of the choices you make? Do I harm anyone? Have I given control of each person's choice to anyone else? What witness do you bear for God?"

"I am miserable and pitiable. No one cares about me. No one helps me. Everyone despises me."

"Is this your evidence, making mockery of his appeal to you, when he has honored you and judged you a worthy witness?"

"But if some person of authority judges you as impious and unholy? How does that affect you?"

"I have been judged impious and unholy."

"Nothing else?"

"Nothing. If he had said that the statement, 'If it is day, it is light,' is false, what happens to the statement? Who is judged? Who is condemned? Who got it wrong – the conditional statement or the person who said it was false?

Don't be disturbed when the ignorant judge you

Well, who is this person to pass such judgement on you? Does he know what piety or impiety is? Has he studied it? Where and from whom? A musician will have no respect for a person who mistakes the highest string for the lowest string on a musical instrument. A mathematician will have no respect for a person who thinks that the same circle will have a different radius at a different point. So how can a truly educated person pay any attention to an uneducated person regarding what is holy or unholy, just, or unjust? How dishonorable of the educated that would be! Is that what you learned here?

Wouldn't you rather leave such quibbles to insignificant people who sit in a corner, receive their small fees or nothing and whine about it? Will you not step forward and practice what you have learned? We don't need any more quibbles – our Stoic texts are full of them. What do we need then? We need people who apply what they have learned and bear witness to it in their actions. I would like you take on this character, so I don't have to use old examples when I teach, and I can use an example of our own.

Who should think about these things? Those who have the time for it. Humans are made for abstract thoughts. Let's not study them in a hurried and distracted way. Sit free of distractions. Listen now to the tragic actor; then to the musician. Don't behave like an escapee who praises the performers while nervously glancing around, ready to be alarmed and disturbed if someone mentions the name of his master. It is shameful for philosophers to study works of nature this way.

We are unable to enjoy life because we are in the grip of emotions

What does "master" mean? No one is master over another but death and life, pleasure, and pain. Without these, bring me the king, you will see how unwavering I am. But when he comes with these things, along with thunder and lightning, then I am afraid. I act as if I am a runaway slave, brought to face his master. Even when I have a break from these things, my attention to the performance is no better than that of the slave's. I wash, drink, and sing but all the while I am afraid and gloomy. But if I free myself from my emotions that make the master frightening, what troubles can I have?

Avoid the temptation to preach to those who cannot understand

Should I then announce this to the entire world? No, because we need to make allowances for the uneducated. We should say to ourselves: "They are telling me what they think is good for themselves. So, I can't blame them."

Thus, Socrates forgave his jailer who wept when he was about to drink poison and said, "How noble you are to weep for me!" He does not say to the jailer, "That's why we wouldn't let the women in!" No, he treats the jailer indulgently as he would a child and says it only to his close friends who can understand it.

Think about this

If you wish any good things, get it from yourself. Discourses I.29.4. Epictetus [WO]

Have These Principles Handy During Difficult Times

Key ideas of this discourse

1. *No matter how powerful an authority we face, there is someone higher looking down upon us.*

2. *The higher authority is pleased when you show what you have learned: Good and evil come from your choices and externals are nothing to you.*

Remember to please the ultimate authority

When you come face to face with a prominent person, remember that there is someone else looking from above. You must please him first. He asks:

"When you were in school, how were you taught to look upon exile, imprisonment, restraint, death, and disgrace?"

"I was taught they are indifferents."

"What do you say now? Have they changed in any way?"

"No."

"Have you changed?"

"No"

"Tell me what 'indifferents' are."

"Whatever we cannot control."

"The bottom line?"

"They are nothing to me."

"Tell me what good things are."

"Making the right choice and using impressions correctly."

"What is the goal of life?"

"To follow you."

"Do you still stand by it?"

"Yes, I do."

See the insignificance of externals

Hold confidently to these convictions and go in. You will see what it is like to be young and educated among those who are not. I hope you have thoughts like these: "Why do we make such elaborate preparations to face what amounts to nothing? Is that what meant by 'authority'? Are the courtyards, the palace staff, and the armed guards just this? Is it for this that I sat though many long lectures? It all amounts to nothing but I was preparing for it as though it were something great."

Think about this

"Define for me what the 'indifferents' are."
   Whatever things we cannot control.
   "Remind me what you thought was good."
   The will and the right use of impressions.

Discourses I.30.3/4. Epictetus [RD]

ABOUT THE AUTHOR

Dr Chuck Chakrapani. He has been a long-term, but embarrassingly inconsistent, practitioner of Stoicism. He is the president of Leger Analytics and a Distinguished Visiting Professor at Ryerson University.

Chuck has authored books on several subjects over the years which include research methods, statistics, and investment strategies. His personal website is ChuckChakrapani.com

His books on Stoicism include *Unshakable Freedom*, *A Fortunate Storm* and *The Good Life Handbook* (a rendering of Epictetus' Enchiridion.)

Also by the Author

A Fortunate Storm

Three unconnected events – a shipwreck in Piraeus, a play in Thebes, and the banishment of a rebel in Turkey – connected three unrelated individuals to give birth to a philosophy. It was to endure 2,000 years.

Get a FREE COPY of the eBook at TheStoicGym.com

The Good Life Handbook

Available in print, digital, and audio editions, *The Good Life Handbook* is a rendering of *Enchiridion* in plain English.

Please get your copy in your favorite online bookstore.

Unshakable Freedom

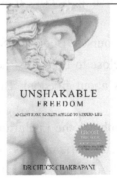

How can we achieve total personal freedom when we have so many obligations and so many demands on our time? Is personal freedom even possible?

Yes, it is possible, said the Stoics.

Stoicism in Plain English

Stoicism in Plain English books 1-5 represent the complete works of Epictetus.

Stoic Foundations (Discourses Book 1) explains the basic tenets of Stoicism.

Stoic Choices is the plain English version of Discourses Book 2. It revolves around themes of choice.

Stoic Training is the third book of *Discourses* of Epictetus in plain English. Stoics did not only believe in theoretical knowledge but held that it is critical we practice what we learned.

Stoic Freedom (Discourses Book 4) focuses on freedom. Personal freedom is close to Epictetus' heart, and his rhetoric shines when he talks about freedom. But, what does a free person look like?

Stoic Inspirations combines the Enchiridion (Epictetus' pupil Arrian's notebook summarizing his teachings) and the remaining fragments of the lost Discourses books. It completes the Stoicism in Plain English series on Epictetus from The Stoic Gym.

Made in United States
Troutdale, OR
11/13/2023